APR 20 '70

The Australian Ballot: *The Story of an American Reform*

The Australian Ballot:

The Story of an American Reform

by L. E. Fredman

Michigan State University Press

1968

To Carolyn and Jacqueline

CONTENTS

PREFACE

By the middle decades of the nineteenth century, it was obvious to many Americans that the manipulation of the ballot box had made voting a meaningless procedure. Political parties provided identifiable, printed ballots, which were issued to voters at the polls. Under this system candidates for office were often required to pay the party excessive sums to insure that their names would be placed on the ballot, and voters were bribed or intimidated by agents of the political machines. Even where the election proceedings were "honest," the voter usually had to face the peril of the long ballot with its list of little known candidates for minor offices. A reform of the ballot system was clearly needed.

To replace oral voting, Britain had in 1872 adopted the method pioneered in her Australian colonies in the 1850's, whereby the government printed and distributed the ballots, accepted nominations, and made elaborate provision for secrecy in the voting. It was this Australian ballot which appealed particularly to that small, high-minded group of reformers usually called Liberals or Mugwumps, as part of their general quest for honest and limited government. Somewhat different motives led other groups, such as the southern Bourbons, Populists and Labor to support the reform. The first Australian ballot law was passed in February, 1888, providing only for elections in the city of Louisville, Kentucky; but a state-wide law, drafted by Richard Henry Dana III, was passed by Massachusetts later in the same year, and other states quickly followed. By the next presidential elections, thirty-eight states had passed Australian ballot laws in one form or another.

The passage and amendment of the Australian ballot was a major reform issue of the 1880's and 1890's. It was part of the general reforming spirit of the age, for many of the same sort of people who advocated ballot reform were also to be found urging civil service and tariff revision. They were, admittedly, genteel reformers, only dimly aware of the social and economic sources of the power of the political machines, but their criticisms of boss rule provided a base upon which the more realistic reformers of the Progressive era could build. However, the distinction between Mugwump and Progressive should not be overworked. Not every Mugwump and ballot reformer became aged and disillusioned like his mentor, E. L. Godkin. The decade of the Pullman Strike and Free Silver is also the decade of the foundation of the National Municipal League. Theodore Roosevelt, who dominated national politics after 1901, had been one of the founders of the City Reform Club in 1882. Seth Low, a reform mayor of greater New York, had been a reform mayor of Brooklyn in 1884, the year in which the word Mugwump was first widely used of those Republicans who bolted from their party after the nomination of James G. Blaine.

Textbooks in political science and history usually mention the Australian ballot, but there are few detailed accounts of the movement which established it. The *Australian Ballot System* by John H. Wigmore, then of the Boston bar, later the famous Dean of the Northwestern University School of Law, was published in 1889 when the movement was scarcely under way, and is understandably brief and polemical. Eldon Cobb Evans' dissertation, *A History of the Australian Ballot System in the United States,* was published in 1917, but it is the work of a political scientist and is primarily concerned with an analysis of ballot legislation before and after the reform. Arthur E. Ludington in 1911 produced his invaluable *American Ballot Laws, 1888–1910,* which is simply a digest. In view of the limited character of these early studies and of several more recent works dealing with the liberal reformers in general, there appears to be adequate justification for a historian and an Australian to tackle the Australian ballot reform in the United States.

One cannot begin with the passage of the first laws in Kentucky and Massachusetts. There are several questions which should be answered first. What is the derivation of the ballot? Where did the Australian and American colonists obtain the idea? And why did the Australian colonists and British reformers want a

Preface

change? These are dealt with in the first chapter. The Australian and British laws provided the contrast and alternative which American reformers, disturbed by the conditions described in the second chapter, had been seeking.

This was of course only one facet of contact between the United States and Australia. The first American vessel visited the penal settlement at Sydney, then only four years old and short of food, with a speculative but welcome cargo of provisions in November, 1792. Other vessels followed in increasing numbers. China traders hoped to obtain specie; sealers and whalers wanted a port in the remote seas; and the immigrants of the 1850's were looking for gold. The "Shenandoah," a fearsome Confederate raider, added to her crew in Melbourne in 1865, and the British government later paid heavily for this negligence. The Great White Fleet received a rapturous welcome in 1908, which foreshadows the later age of war and postwar alliance in the Pacific. Individual American immigrants include J. C. Williamson, actor and founder of the dominant theatrical firm which still bears his name; James Rutherford, pioneer of inland transport, who for fifty years ran the coaching firm of Cobb and Co.; and Walter Birley Griffin, probably the most creative architect to work in Australia, who laid out the national capital of Canberra. Australians have borrowed heavily from the United States for their technology and entertainment, and their constitution was greatly influenced by the earlier federal constitution of the United States. The contacts and borrowing, like the trade between the two countries, have been one-sided. However, three pieces of Australian social engineering, to use the phrase of the distinguished jurist, Roscoe Pound, have been considered for borrowing by Americans. Henry Demarest Lloyd about 1900 spoke highly of industrial arbitration in Australia and New Zealand, but the compulsory and judicial features have appealed to few Americans. The system of transfer of land by registration on title, devised by Robert Torrens in South Australia in 1858, was widely copied in the United States. Laws permitting the system were passed in nineteen states between 1897 and 1919. However, several have been repealed and it has never taken hold except in a few metropolitan centers such as Los Angeles. The third instance is the Australian ballot which has been well and truly borrowed as it has been adopted by name in every state. This should be more widely known, if only to modify the common impression that Australia can export only wool (subject to the American tariff), singers and sportsmen.

The author would especially like to thank a number of scholars, officials and librarians: Mr. R. Becker and Dr. J. R. Kantor of the Bancroft Library, Berkeley; Dr. R. W. Hill of the New York Public Library; Dr. R. W. Roalfe of the Northwestern University School of Law; Miss Maurine Brunner of the Michigan State Library and Miss Geneva Kebler of the Michigan Historical Commission, Lansing; Dr. Clyde Walton of the Illinois State Historical Library, Springfield; Mr. Richard S. Childs of the National Municipal League; Mr. Milton Small, Supervisor of Secondary Education, Boise; Mr. Wade O. Martin, Jr., Secretary of State, Louisiana; Mr. Frank Jordan, Secretary of State, California; Mr. F. L. Ley, Chief Commonwealth Electoral Officer, Canberra; Miss Evangeline Lynch, Louisiana State University Library; and Dr. Henry C. Dethloff, University of Southwestern Louisiana.

CHAPTER I

A Spirited Contest

"Spirited contest, my dear Sir," said the little man. "I am
delighted to hear it," said Mr. Pickwick, rubbing his hands.
"I like to see sturdy patriotism, on whatever side it is called
forth;—and so it's a spirited contest?" "Oh yes," said the
little man, "very much so indeed. We have opened all the
public houses in the place, and left our adversary nothing
but the beer shops—masterly stroke of policy that, my dear
Sir, eh?"—and the little man smiled complacently and took
a large pinch of snuff.

(Charles Dickens, 1837)

This open or American Ballot then, as giving no protection
to the voter, was not established in Victoria.

(Hugh C. E. Childers, 1860)

The derivation of the world "ballot," according to the *Oxford
English Dictionary,* is the Italian *ballotta,* or little ball. The word
was first used in the mid-sixteenth century in a history of Italy,
and meant the ball itself, or the system of secret voting using
colored balls, beans or other objects. Such a system had been
known to the ancient world. The fellow-citizens of Pericles cast
black or white stones in giving the verdict of the popular courts.
In Rome, the three *Leges Tabellariae,* passed between 139 and
131 B.C., introduced secret voting for the *Comitia Centuriata.* The
citizen received a number of wooden tablets each engraved with
the name of a candidate, or with "yea" or "nay" when the *Comitia*
was acting in its judicial capacity; whereupon he cast one and
returned the others to the officials. Such methods did not curb
astute and free-spending political bosses, whether in Caesar's Rome
or the Florence of the Medici. But the ballot worked sufficiently
well for the system and the word to be copied in medieval England.[1]

[1] Charles Dickens, *The Posthumous Papers of the Pickwick Club* (London, 1837), 120–33; Hansard's *Parliamentary Debates,* third series, CLVI

The Australian Ballot:

Although copied, the ballot was never widespread in England and was confined to local and company elections. Some places persisted with colored balls and peas, while others began to use pen and paper. The new charter of Pontrefact in 1607, for example, provided that the mayor be elected by writing the desired name on a scroll, upon which they were collected, counted and destroyed. Many of the future colonists of America and Australia undoubtedly saw the ballot used in such elections in their native England. In 1835, the Municipal Corporations Act abolished the motley array of voting methods and required open and uniform voting.[2]

Two years later, Dickens' Mr. Pickwick and his friends were observing the epic and fictional struggle between the Buffs and the Blues to elect a representative for "that ancient, loyal and patriotic borough" of Eatanswill. The ballot had never been used in parliamentary elections, which now followed a fairly standard procedure. On the appointed day, a wooden structure called a "hustings" was erected, and the clerk read the writ and called for candidates. They came forward and addressed the crowd from this hustings or platform, which later acquired a second meaning as a synonym for the policy of a candidate or party. If the candidate or candidates were equal to the number to be elected, they were so declared; but if there was a contest, a poll was conducted then or at a later date, and by open and oral voting. The qualifications were complex and very restrictive. But whether he had a vote or not, the average citizen could cheer and participate, for election day was usually a holiday and the contestants were usually very liberal. They provided bands and banners and all the para-

---

(February 9, 1860), 789; Richard Henry Dana, "The Practical Working of the Australian System of Voting in Massachusetts," *Annals of the American Academy of Political and Social Science,* II (May, 1892), 733–34; Harold F. Gosnell, "Ballot," in E. R. A. Seligman and A. Johnson eds., *Encyclopaedia of the Social Sciences,* 15 vols. (New York, 1930–35), II, 410.

[2] Charles Gross, "The Early History of the Ballot in England," *American Historical Review,* III (April, 1898), 456–63. He mentions the use of a ballot at only one parliamentary election, for Lymington in 1577. *Ibid.,* 459–60.

phernalia of a "spirited contest." The expense was great, but there was no lack of candidates willing and able to buy a vote or stand a treat or to hire a few bullies to do the work more effectively. In the borough of Horsham in 1847, the liquor ran free for six weeks, and when this failed some of the electors were abducted. The estimated cost to each candidate here was anything up to one hundred thousand pounds. This was no isolated example. H. J. Hanham has estimated from the trial of Election Petitions that between 1865 and 1884, at least sixty-four English boroughs, returning one hundred thirteen members, or nearly one-fifth of the House of Commons were undoubtedly corrupt. Sometimes the corruption was more quietly and systematically arranged, and based on the social influence of the great county landlords. As late as 1868, Edward Fellowes of Huntingdonshire was accustomed to riding grimly up to the polls with one hundred fifty tenants in serried and instructed ranks behind him. They quietly watched while he was returned unopposed.[3]

What of elections in the British colonies beyond the seas? By 1850, the former penal settlement of Australia, established in 1788, was of great and growing importance. The Australian Colonies Government Act had just been passed, separating Port Phillip from New South Wales under the name of Victoria, and providing that the legislative councils of the four colonies could draw up their own constitutions for approval by the Imperial parliament. The old Legislative Council of Victoria passed the first Australian ballot law amid all the turmoil and social dislocation of the Gold Rush and before the introduction of responsible government. The law was put into effect in time for the election of the first parliament under her new constitution in September, 1856.[4]

[3] Dickens, *Pickwick*, 120–33; Charles Seymour, *Electoral Reform in England and Wales: the Development and Operation of the Parliamentary Franchise, 1832–85* (New Haven, 1915), 205–06; W. I. Jennings, *Appeal to the People* (London, 1960), 105–06; H. J. Hanham, *Elections and Party Management: Politics in the Time of Gladstone and Disraeli* (London, 1959), 4, 262–83.

[4] The Australian Colonies Government Act of 1850 gave the new colony of Victoria, also Van Dieman's Land [now Tasmania] and South Aus-

The Australian Ballot:

As now understood, the terms secret ballot and Australian ballot are interchangeable. It is not possible to trace the precise origin of the idea. Some immigrants were undoubtedly familiar with its use in local elections in Britain before 1835. Others may have been familiar with the crusade of George Grote for ballot reform in the 1830's. It had also been one of the six radical political reforms of the Chartist platform. Furthermore, the new and fast-growing pastoral settlement of Port Phillip was accustomed to frequent public meetings to air a variety of grievances, and in particular to protest the continuation of government from distant Sydney.

There was some dispute as to whether local elections were so corrupt that they contributed to the demand for ballot reform. One must bear in mind that former Australian politicians offering evidence in Britain were anxious to support the reform there, and to emphasize the contrast between the old and new elections in Australia. Thus, Robert Torrens, former premier of South Australia and now the Liberal Member of Parliament for Cambridge, said in 1869: "We had there bribery, a great deal of rioting, and broken heads, and broken panes of glass, and of smashing windows; exactly the same thing that goes on in this country, though, perhaps, more aggravated frequently than it is in England." Another Liberal member was Hugh Childers who had been Victorian Commissioner for Trade and Customs when the reform was passed. In his maiden speech in 1860, he said that the old colonial elections had been orderly but marred by treating in

tralia, a form of government similar to that given to New South Wales in 1842. The Legislative Council of the latter or mother colony would determine the numbers and electoral districts of the first Victorian Legislative Council. The lieutenant-governor of Victoria (Sir Charles Hotham was commissioned as governor in 1855) accordingly had wide powers. He nominated his Executive Council and one-third of the Legislative Council; he had a power of veto, a permanent civil list and control of the land revenue; all bills could and certain bills had to be reserved for the assent of the Imperial government. Two-thirds of the Legislative Council was elected, with a high property qualification for voters and members. The colonists continued to agitate for "responsible government," meaning that the membership and policy of the Executive should be dependent upon a parliamentary majority.

The terms Britain and British will henceforth be used for convenience, and embody the formation of the United Kingdom in 1801.

the towns. Two agents-general—Sir George Verdon of Victoria and an early supporter, Francis Dutton of South Australia—also offered opinions. Verdon considered that the property qualifications and the newness of social relations left little scope for the British type of bribery and influence. Dutton cited the quite modest range of two thousand to four thousand pounds as an excessive expenditure for an election. In any event, conditions in general could not have been worse than in Britain.[5]

During the course of the agitation for separation, a public meeting was held in Melbourne on March 21, 1851, with William Nicholson, mayor of Melbourne in the chair, to draw up a petition to the Legislative Council of New South Wales. The chief resolution recommended that the first Legislative Council of Victoria should be elected by equal electoral districts; and the fourth resolution urged "the principle of vote by ballot." These resolutions passed by large majorities. The speakers seemed more concerned about the unsavory example of British elections than any present danger in their own midst, though local examples were brought forward. The petition had no effect, and the first Victorian council was elected later in the year by a system which favored the squatters and their broad acres.[6]

The heavy immigration of the next few years greatly increased

[5] "Report of the Select Committee on Parliamentary and Municipal Elections," (hereinafter referred to as the *Hartington Committee*), *Sessional Papers, House of Commons*, VIII (1868–69), Q. 8728–36 (Torrens), 9127–34 (Dutton), 9810–25 (Verdon); Hansard's *Parliamentary Debates*, third series, CLVI (February 9, 1860), 787–89; Geoffrey Serle, *The Golden Age: a History of the Colony of Victoria, 1851–61* (Melbourne, 1963), 208. The conclusion reached in Serle's thorough work supports the contemporary views of Childers and Verdon.

In the year of his premiership, 1857, Robert Richard Torrens (1814–84) introduced the famous system of land transfer by registration on title which bears his name. Hoping to introduce it in Britain, he served in parliament from 1868 to 1874. Hugh Culling Eardley Childers (1827–96) was a member from 1860 to 1885 and from 1886 to 1896, serving in each of Gladstone's ministries.

[6] Melbourne *Argus*, March 22, 24, 1851. The term "squatter" which originally meant an illegal occupant as in the United States was being used by 1850, as it is today, to describe a grazier with a large holding. The *Argus* was their bitter opponent, and gave the meeting one page of a four-page issue.

the influence of the town radicals, but there was no constitutional means of directing the policy of the autocratic governor, Sir Charles Hotham, and his Executive Council. They had been appointed by the governor to the chief offices and sat in the Legislative Council as his nominees. When the new constitution arrived from Britain, Hotham considered rightly or wrongly that he must immediately introduce responsible government. The members of the Executive Council resigned on November 27, 1855; and on the following day, William Haines, the former Colonial Secretary, notified the Legislative Council that the governor had asked him to form the first ministry under responsible government. A Minute was also read in which the governor said that he expected future ministers to continue to uphold his views. Hotham was already under a cloud because of his handling of the forcible resistance to the gold license fee during the previous year. Four members of the old executive had a pecuniary interest in his action as the new constitution gave them generous pensions if they were "released from office on political grounds." If they awaited the elections and the meeting of the first parliament, they might be defeated and jeopardize their pensions. Having secured their future by resigning, the former executive of an unpopular governor now claimed to be a responsible ministry backed by a majority in the Council. Their regular opponents were determined to prove them wrong.

On December 4, a motion to censure the government was defeated by only one vote. Then on December 18, Nicholson moved, "That in the opinion of this House any new Electoral Act should provide for electors recording their vote by secret ballot." He too seemed primarily concerned with the faults of British elections, and his practical proposals included little more than a separate room for the ballot box and colored boxes for illiterates, which would hardly be secret. Haines asked for proof of local bribery and readily picked holes in the suggested plan. The motion was passed by thirty-three votes to twenty-five, with the ministry and conservative members voting against it. Haines accepted the practices of responsible government by tendering his resignation for a second time. Accordingly, the mover of the motion had to play the part of a Leader of the Opposition without a real party behind him. Nicholson was vainly trying to form a ministry when Hotham died on December 31. The lieutenant-governor had no choice but to recall Haines who indicated that the ministry would now treat the ballot as an open question. They might oppose but would not stake their life on this section of the Electoral Bill. In this uncertain situation a new figure appeared on the scene.[7]

Henry Samuel Chapman was one of those educated and adventurous Englishmen who lived in and wrote about various parts of the Empire, and made a considerable contribution to the development of Canada, New Zealand, Tasmania and Victoria. In Britain, he had written pamphlets urging manhood suffrage and the repeal of the Corn Laws, and he later resigned from his post as Colonial Secretary of Tasmania because of his opposition to Transportation. It is not surprising that he usually voted with the radical side and for Nicholson's motion in the old Victorian Legislative Council. He drafted the Ballot clauses which became part of the Electoral Act passed on March 19, 1856.[8]

The Australian ballot was embodied in law for the first time as several sections of a statute entitled "An Act to provide for the Election of Members to serve in the Legislative Council and Legislative Assembly of Victoria respectively. (Assented to 19th March, 1856)." It was published as a supplement to the Victorian

[7] *Ibid.*, December 19, 1855, January 17, 1856; William Westgarth, *The Colony of Victoria* (London, 1864), 161–69; Serle, *Golden Age*, 200–03. Haines is regarded officially as the first premier of Victoria appointed on November 28, 1855, in these odd circumstances. Nicholson sat in the old Council between 1852 and 1856, and was premier in 1859–60.

[8] Henry Samuel Chapman (1803–81) was a journalist and politician in Canada (1823–34); judge in New Zealand (1844–52); colonial secretary of Tasmania (1852–54); barrister and politician in Victoria and twice attorney-general (1854–62); judge in Victoria (1862–64); and judge in New Zealand (1864–75). Chapman personally had mixed fortunes under the new electoral law, being twice defeated before entering Parliament. See obituary in Melbourne *Argus*, December 29, 1881, and R. S. Neale, "H. S. Chapman and the 'Victorian' Ballot," *Historical Studies*, XII (April, 1967), 506–21, who has had access to MS sources and supersedes previous accounts.

Government Gazette of March 26. Though extended to local government elections in 1861 and revised on points of detail, the law remains substantially unaltered.[9]

After provisions dealing with the appointment of registrars and returning officers, and the compiling of lists of electors, the Act provided that the returning officer should erect a booth or hire rooms, at least one for every six hundred electors, and divide the same into several compartments. One or more compartments were to be equipped for marking ballot papers. Only the elector recording his vote, the returning officers, clerks and scrutineers representing the candidates were allowed to enter. Any other person who entered was guilty of a misdemeanor. The Writ calling for representatives to attend a new parliament was read on the nomination day, and if a contest was required, it was held on the day set down in the Writ and included only the candidates proposed on nomination day. The returning officer was then responsible for printing the ballot papers in a set form, signing them upon the back, and delivering a sufficient number to deputies at each booth. Having received a ballot paper signed upon the back, the elector retired to an inner compartment and there struck out the names of candidates he did not wish to vote for and then deposited the folded paper in a locked box in the presence of the officials. The officials could mark papers for incapacitated persons. No papers were to be removed from the room. The ballot was also endorsed with the elector's number on the roll and his name checked off which was *prima facie* evidence of his having voted. Necessary expenses were to be paid out of the consolidated revenue of the colony.[10]

In the "Introductory Sketch" to his book on the Australian ballot system written in 1889, John H. Wigmore, then a twenty-six-year-old Boston lawyer anxious to boost this emerging reform, described Francis S. Dutton of South Australia as "the father of

---

[9] In 1890, the statute law of Victoria was consolidated for the first time, and the subject matter of Elections was placed in part five of the Constitution Act Amendments Act.

[10] *Election Act,* Sections 33–38, 55, and Schedule F.

the measure." This assertion is repeated in many articles and editorials on the subject including a brief, undated pamphlet in the Mitchell Library attributed to Fred Johns, a South Australian journalist prominent about fifty years ago, entitled, *The Australian Ballot. Pioneered by South Australia. Historic Movement*. On the other hand, Ernest Scott, an Englishman who held the chair of history at the University of Melbourne for twenty-five years, asserted that the Chartists and the public meeting held in March, 1851, had preceded the actions of Dutton. The question is not worth considering in terms of interstate rivalry. The principle of the ballot was old, even in Britain; what was new was a detailed measure applicable to modern conditions. For this Victoria, and Nicholson and Chapman in particular, must receive the credit. The main speaker at the Melbourne meeting of 1851 stated that South Australia had "preceded" them in taking up the question seriously; and, in both colonies in 1851, the Legislative Councils rejected petitions. The first law in South Australia to include the secret ballot was passed in April, 1856, a month later than that of Victoria. Dutton had been its persistent champion. Later, as agent-general for his state, he was able to give evidence on its operation to the Hartington Committee on Parliamentary and Municipal Elections in 1869.[11]

South Australia introduced the method, later adopted in the United States, of voting for a candidate by marking a cross within a square alongside his name on the ballot; whereas Victoria for many years clung to the system in Chapman's law of striking out the names of candidates not voted for.

[11] J. H. Wigmore, *The Australian Ballot System as Embodied in the Legislation of Various Countries* (Boston, 1889), 1–57; R. H. Dana, "Sir William Vernon Harcourt and the Australian Ballot Law," *Proceedings of the Massachusetts Historical Society*, LVIII (June, 1925), 413; Boston *Daily Advertiser*, November 4, 1889 (sample editorial crediting Dutton); Melbourne *Argus*, March 8, 24, 1851; Ernest Scott, "The History of the Victorian Ballot," *Victorian Historical Magazine*, VIII (November, 1920), 1–14. Johns's pamphlet has no author or publication details. Eldon C. Evans mistakenly gives the text of a South Australian Act of 1858 as "the original Australian Ballot Act." *A History of the Australian Ballot System in the United States* (Chicago, 1917), Appendix A.

The Australian Ballot:

There is little doubt that the new system virtually terminated bribery, lavish treating, and disorder at elections. This was the considered opinion of William Westgarth and Thomas McCombie, the two early historians of Victoria, who both served as returning officers under the new law, and also of Dutton and Torrens of South Australia. However, Torrens, as an active partisan of the reform in the House of Commons, was probably exaggerating the faults of the old elections in Australia.[12]

Even the new system was not perfect, however. In their replies to Lord Kimberley's circular letter of September 30, 1870, the ministers in Queensland and New South Wales said false personation was still a problem. Governor Charles Du Cane of Tasmania described the "Tasmanian Dodge," which was also known as the "Simpson System," devised by James Simpson, editor of the Hobart *Mercury*. The party agent lined up his followers and sent the first into the polling place to vote a blank and bring out a ballot. He was then paid the agreed sum. The agent filled in the ballot and gave it to his second voter who deposited it and brought out another ballot in turn. He was paid and the voting proceeded down the line with the loss of only the first member. Du Cane hastened to add that it was never proved that the system was actually used in Tasmania. Nevertheless the prospect gave rise to various schemes to ensure that the ballot deposited was the ballot received. Sir James McCulloch, the Victorian premier, explained their system in which the returning officer placed the voter's number on the back of his ballot. He said that it was an offense to compare a number on the ballot with a number and name on the roll when the boxes were opened and so secrecy was not endangered. Later, American draftsmen of ballot statutes suffered torments trying to devise stubs, numbers, and other procedures to avert what seemed a fanciful reminder of the unusual

---

12 Westgarth, *Colony of Victoria*, 171–72; Thomas McCombie, *History of the Colony of Victoria from its Settlement to the Death of Sir Charles Hotham* (Melbourne, 1858), 291. McCombie had spoken at the earlier meeting. Melbourne *Argus*, March 24, 1851. See also the *Hartington Committee*, as cited in footnote 5, above.

fauna of the tiny island—the Tasmanian Wolf and the Tasmanian Devil.[13]

While the measure was being passed and well received in the Australian colonies, its chances had declined in Britain. Between 1833 and 1839, George Grote, one of the leaders of the considerable body of parliamentary radicals, had presented six motions in favor of the ballot, and on the last occasion attracted two hundred sixteen votes to the opposition's three hundred thirty-three. It was evident from Grote's wide range of arguments that he regarded the ballot as the first step in a complete scheme of political reform. He proposed that manhood suffrage should be steadily introduced over a period of twenty years; there should be equal districts each of one member, annually elected; and the poll should be taken by secret ballot at several places on the same day. It would be pointless to extend the franchise, he added, just to increase the numbers dependent on their landlords or pushed aside by their hirelings.[14]

After 1839, Grote tended to lose interest. The revolutionary aims of some of the Chartists whose platform included the ballot discredited any alternative to the traditional open voting. Critics also claimed that the ballot had failed to achieve secrecy and order in American elections. The author of *Is the Ballot a Mistake?* quoted a New York newspaper with relish:

> Mr. Eley, a merchant in Maiden Lane, was severely wounded yesterday in the sixth ward. In making his escape he was pursued by a gang of ruffians, and was compelled to rush into a

[13] "Papers Relative to the Operation of the System of the Ballot in the Colonies," *Sessional Papers, House of Commons,* XLVII (1871), 317. The letters were replies to a circular letter sent by the colonial secretary, Lord Kimberley, on September 30, 1870.

[14] For his speeches in the House of Commons and a pamphlet written in 1831, see George Grote, *Minor Works, with Critical Remarks on his Intellectual Character, Writings and Speeches, by Alexander Bain* (London, 1873), 1–55. Grote's major work was a widely read, multi-volume history of Greece (1846–56). Chapman was connected with the Philosophical Radicals such as Grote and J. A. Roebuck and their causes when in England between 1835 and 1843. See R. S. Neale, "H. S. Chapman and the 'Victorian' Ballot," 509–15.

house to save his life. It proved to be the residence of a Mr. _____, a Customs-house officer. He complained that it was very rude for a stranger to come into his house without an invitation.

In such a case, it was evidently felt that even an English gentleman would condone the breach of manners. Opponents also argued that bribery would continue because the secret voters could now take payment from both sides, or a candidate's agent would place bets with the voters, for example laying one pound to a shilling that his man's opponent would win. He was virtually bribing the voter to vote for his man and giving him an incentive to do it, though secret. They said that the mother country could learn little from her young and inexperienced Australian colonies. Most of the leading politicians on both sides opposed it. So did John Stuart Mill who by the 1860's was one of the most influential philosophers and reformers in the English-speaking world. He contended that the restricted franchise was not a right but a duty and should be exercised publicly and in accordance with the voter's most conscientious opinion of the public good.[15]

On February 9, 1860, during the course of the agitation, a private member sought leave to introduce a bill providing for vote by ballot in the boroughs of Wakefield and Gloucester. Viscount Palmerston, the prime minister, expressed his well-known opposition. When he sat down, Hugh Childers rose to make an unexpected and very fine maiden speech. He explained the operation and beneficial results of the ballot in Victoria. It protected the voter by giving him secrecy; whereas the American ballot had been established not for secrecy but for speed, which had been made necessary by manhood suffrage and frequent

[15] New York *Commercial Advertiser,* April 9, 1834, quoted in S. C. Denison, *Is the Ballot a Mistake?* (London, 1838), 124; *Edinburgh Review,* CXII (July, 1860), 270, 283–84; John Stuart Mill, *Considerations on Representative Government* (London, 1861), 298–312 in the Everyman edition. See Hansard's *Parliamentary Debates,* third series, CCVII (June 26, 1871), 594–604, for one of the better Conservative speeches. Torrens told the Hartington Committee that his opposition in South Australia was based on the views of Mill and Palmerston.

elections. Childers's speech was to no avail. The motion was defeated by one hundred eighteen votes to one hundred forty-nine.[16]

Eight years later, a greatly enlarged electorate returned a firm Liberal majority under William Ewart Gladstone. However, thirty-four petitions were presented to the judges who under a recent law had replaced the authority of the House of Commons over contested elections. Such corruption was disclosed that John Bright and other radicals in the party demanded action. A Select Committee on Parliamentary and Municipal Elections appointed March, 1869, with the Marquis of Hartington as chairman, presented its report late in July. Witnesses described the use of the ballot in several colonies, the United States, France, Italy and Greece; and Torrens and Dutton spoke at first hand of the agitation and improvement in South Australia. The general impression created by this evidence offered a sharp contrast with the conduct of British elections and the Report recommended the adoption of the ballot, if actually secret. There was one curious note: a witness told the Committee that the citizens of the small town of Maryport were claiming that the Australian colonies had copied the ballot from them as they had used the system in local elections. As to how this came about, he was not at all clear. On the other hand, Dutton in his evidence had loftily taken the credit for himself. Soon afterwards, Lord Hartington and William E. Forster were able to watch the operation of a secret ballot to elect the first members of the London School Board. The procedure was so novel that one of their own colleagues in the Cabinet voted and then asked the returning officer where he was to sign his name. Accustomed to signing the poll-book, he absentmindedly wanted to sign the ballot paper.[17]

[16] Hansard's *Parliamentary Debates,* third series, CLVI (February 9, 1860), 771–95.

[17] *Hartington Committee,* Q. 9167 (Dutton), 9955ff. (A. S. Hankel, formerly of Charleston, South Carolina), 12158–60 (Taylor and Maryport) ; T. Wemyss Reid, *Life of the Rt. Hon. William Edward Forster,* 2 vols. (London, 1888), II, 3–4.

The Australian Ballot:

On May 9, 1870, Hartington introduced the government's bill to carry out the Committee's recommendations. There was already a private member's bill on the notice-paper, but neither received much attention before the session closed. The key to the situation was the prime minister who in this and other matters was growing more radical with the years. He had voted against Grote's motions in the 1830's and reaffirmed his opposition in 1866. An entry in his diary for July 27, 1870, indicated mixed feelings: "H. of C. Spoke on ballot, and voted in 324–230 with mind satisfied, and as to feeling, a lingering reluctance." The Cabinet was re-shuffled before the session of 1871, and Forster, the Vice-President of the Council, was included expressly to guide the new Ballot Bill. He introduced it on February 20, 1871, and it finally passed the House of Commons on August 8 after twenty-seven sittings. Speaking for the bill, Forster stated tersely that the ballot was the only way to check bribery and intimidation. A secret vote would weaken the influence exploited by wealth, but enable the voter to respond more readily to a "legitimate" influence due to education and service. Unlike Hartington, he urged the House to adopt a completely secret method without stubs or checks. Although the principles of the reform had been canvased for many years and had received a lengthy discussion in the lower House, the Lords claimed that there was insufficient time to consider it. The necessary motion was moved by the venerable and nonpartisan Lord Shaftesbury and obtained a two-to-one majority. The session then closed in August. In a way Forster had asked for this by deliberately stating that the arguments were too well known to need elaboration. Benjamin Disraeli, the Conservative leader, was able to provoke laughter and make debating points by claiming that Forster's statement proved that the question was obsolete.[18]

Perhaps the most unusual M. P. to be unseated about this time was Sir John Acton, later Lord Acton, the famous historian. He was a rather silent member for an Irish seat between 1859 and 1865; after re-election for another Irish seat, he was unseated early in the following year because his agent had used bribery and corruption.

[18] Hansard's *Parliamentary Debates,* third series, CCI (May 9, 1870), 431–46) (Hartington), CCIV (February 20, 1871), 529–47 (Forster),

Twelve months after his first attempt, Forster introduced the bill which became the Ballot Act of 1872. It lingered in committee for some weeks and then faced the gauntlet of the Lords. They offered two main amendments: that the voter should have an option between secret and open voting; and that the ballot should be numbered to allow a later scrutiny of disputed votes, as in Victoria. The Commons had included assistance for illiterates, but naturally regarded any extension of this as a blow to the whole principle. They reluctantly accepted the scrutiny, but refused any other changes of substance. After a brief trial of strength between the Houses, the bill received the Royal assent on July 18.[19]

Generally, the discussion of this Act in parliament produced little that was new. It was not a notable debate. The Conservatives emphasized that there was small demand for it and that the system had received inadequate trial in young and egalitarian Australia. Several followed Mill's warning that it was dangerous and novel to make the vote a personal right—not a privilege or trust. The voter would have greater cause to sell it. Why, the very government did not trust him, one speaker argued sarcastically. He claimed, "That is the estimate the Prime Minister has of the conscientious voter; he wishes the pencil to be tied by a strong piece of tape—red tape, I suppose—for fear he should carry it

CCVII (July 13, 1871), 1667–68 (Disraeli), CCVIII (August 10, 1871), 1264–67 (Shaftesbury). Gladstone's biographer is very sarcastic concerning the House of Lords. John Morley, *The Life of William Ewart Gladstone,* 3 vols. (New York, 1903), II, 366–69.

Forster too had changed his views on purely practical grounds, and retained doubts of principle. He was a minister but did not join the Cabinet until July, 1870, and is best known for guiding the Education Act of that year. Reid, *Forster,* I, 530. On the other hand, Disraeli had supported the ballot when he first stood for Parliament unsuccessfully as a radical in 1832.

The voting cited by Gladstone casts doubt on the statements by Seymour and others that the House was unenthusiastic. Seymour, *Electoral Reform,* 429–32.

[19] Hansard's *Parliamentary Debates,* third series, CCIX (February 8, 1872), 172 (Forster). The London *Times,* June 29, 1872, urged that the opportunity should have been taken to disfranchise the illiterate, which is an interesting anticipation of later American problems and a later American conservative response.

away." Furthermore, the Conservatives were not only alarmed by stolen pencils. A vote by right could be extended to all men, and so it proved. As in the United States, the Australian ballot helped to open up a long series of future reforms.[20]

The Act resembled the Australian laws in most particulars. Candidates were proposed by written nomination and if a contest was necessary, a date was set for a poll. The candidate required only two registered voters to propose and second him and eight to assent to the nomination—ten in all. The poll was to be held within three or six days of the close of nominations, for boroughs and counties respectively. The voters received paper ballots and took them to adjoining compartments where they marked them by a cross opposite the name of the candidate of their choice. The presiding officer could assist illiterate or incapacitated persons. Various offenses were specified, such as the removal of the blank ballot required by the "Tasmanian Dodge." The other check was the printed number on the back of the ballot and its perforated counterfoil. When the ballot was handed over, the voter's number was written on the foil. In theory a voter could be traced; but it was a cumbersome operation to get his number from the roll, scan the foils for the printed number, and then find the ballot, and hardly likely to be abused. The British act thus drew a numbering check from the Victorian act and the cross mark from South Australia. But what it drew from neither and so weakened the law was the system of financing the elections.[21]

The deposit required under the Australian laws was a nominal sum to discourage sham candidates. It was an actual deposit, returnable if the candidate obtained a certain proportion of the votes. But in Britain, the deposit was a high one to cover the costs

[20] Hansard's *Parliamentary Debates,* third series, CCVII (June 26, 1871), 574–77 (Gathorne-Hardy), 594–604 (Hope).

[21] Wigmore, *Australian Ballot,* 90–127 (Ballot Act), and 76, 87–88, 160. The nomination papers required two persons in South Australia, six in Queensland, and ten in Victoria. This offered a stark contrast with the later American practice. Though Wigmore writing in 1889 made some comment, he had not seen what party bosses were really capable of in using the nomination requirements.

or a large part of the costs of the election. By the British Parliamentary Elections Act of 1875, candidates were liable for these expenses and the returning officer could demand security from them.[22]

It would be wrong to claim too much for the ballot. Disorderly scenes and open intimidation of tenants and workmen almost disappeared. Flagrant bribery was obviously now a chancy business. But the more subtle forms of bribery and treating continued to flourish, and thus the ballot was only *one* step in the long campaign against corruption in elections. The contest of 1880 was the first fought by the organized parties and leaders on a national scale; and although it was an orderly election, some candidates spent enormous sums in their partisan eagerness. One unsuccessful candidate spent the equivalent of £6.11.10 a vote, yet Gladstone was returned at Leeds for the equivalent of one-and-four pence. Apart from the candidates, the modern system of directing the campaign and spending large sums through the central party headquarters was beginning about this time. The subsequent trial of twenty-eight election petitions and the unseating of sixteen members for bribery led to the passage of the Corrupt Practices Act of 1883, the basis of the modern law. Each candidate had to appoint an agent to handle his funds and the agent had to file with the returning officer a statement of all receipts and expenses arising from the election. Expenses were strictly limited according to the number of electors. Any two voters could take a petition to court, and the penalties included loss of seat, fine or imprisonment. Corrupt practices and illegal practices were defined. So there was a strong inducement for all candidates and for the parties to obey the law and check needless expense.[23]

[22] *Ibid.,* 160. The radicals' proposal that elections be directly charged against the rates was defeated in the House. Cornelius O'Leary, *The Elimination of Corrupt Practices in British Elections, 1868–1911* (Oxford, 1962), 74–85. At this time, 1889, no deposit was required in South Australia, but twenty pounds was required in Queensland, and fifty to one hundred pounds in Victoria. The first American law for the city of Louisville required a twenty-dollar deposit, but this was abandoned as the system spread.

[23] O'Leary, *Corrupt Practices,* 88–90, 156–58; Seymour, *Electoral Re-*

The Australian Ballot:

If some figures given by the American reformer, William Mills Ivins, are even approximately accurate, the cost of British elections fell remarkably. In 1880, the expenditures were £3,000,000 in 419 constituencies; in 1886, but £624,000 in 442 constituencies with many more voters. In the latter year, only three petitions alleging corrupt practices were presented.[24]

The general election of 1880 produced an even more significant result in Ireland. The Home Rule party controlled most of the seats, but was dominated by the large landlords and Whigs whose policy was suspect to the militant faction led by Charles Parnell. The secret ballot now checked intimidation of the impoverished tenants by the landlords of all parties. The Conservatives lost seats to the Home Rulers and new Parnellites were elected even against the official candidates of their party. Soon afterward, their leader was elected parliamentary chairman and the struggle for independence entered a new phase. The political power of the Irish landlord had been greatly weakened, but disorderly scenes long persisted at the elections.[25]

Corruption in British elections had been a common habit and expectation for many people, and to virtually remove it in a generation was a great achievement. A Royal Commission in 1906 found five hundred venal voters in Worcester, but this sort of thing was rare and the price had slipped to half-a-crown. The Ballot Act had helped to produce this result, along with the Corrupt Practices Act and the disappearance of many small, corruptible constituencies in the redistribution of 1885. These great political reforms together with other measures of the preceding sixty years such as the repeal of the Corn Laws; the Trevelyan-Northcott report on a civil service; the abolition of Purchase in the Army; and the extension of the franchise—all tended to

---

form, 432–34; Louise Overacker and Victor West, *Money in Elections* (New York, 1932), 212–18.

24 William Mills Ivins, *Machine Politics and Money in Elections* (New York, 1887), 148–49.

25 O'Leary, *Corrupt Practices*, 124–28, 228fn.; Conor Cruise O'Brien, *Parnell and his Party, 1880–90* (Oxford, 1957), 1–35.

weaken the power and influence of a landed oligarchy and create
the bases for a representative democracy in Great Britain.[26]

---

[26] O'Leary, *Corrupt Practices,* 229–33; Hanham, *Elections and Party
Management,* 281–83. Both authors emphasize the element of habit.

Forty years after he had fought for the measure in the House, George
Grote offered a sceptical comment when it at length passed—he said
that it would have small effect on elections or party numbers. Morley,
Gladstone, II, 370. Possibly, he was anticipating the gross expenditures
of 1880, and the persistence of several hopelessly corrupt constituencies
until 1885. The unintimidated and enfranchised masses did not hasten
to vote for the Liberals, supposedly the more radical party. The Conservatives were in office for more than twenty of the thirty years following the elections of 1874.

CHAPTER II

Song of the Shoulder-Striker

Knives were drawn and freely used, revolvers discharged
with a perfect recklessness . . . . The police had they interfered would have stood a chance of being annihilated.
(Report of a Democratic party primary,
San Francisco, 1854)

The System contemplated by this bill is a mongrel one,
which has not been tested by experience.
(Veto message of Governor David B.
Hill of New York, 1888)[1]

As the American colonists were familiar with the use of the ballot
in local and company elections in England, they were ready to
adopt it in their new country. The General Court used written
papers to elect the governor of Massachusetts in 1634. Writing
was unusual, however, and the freemen of the Court and the
tything-men (or constables) were for some time elected by casting corn or beans. In 1647 a new and comprehensive election law
required "writing the names of persons elected, in papers open,
or once foulded, not twisted or rouled, that they may be the
sooner perused." The practice spread slowly. All but one of the
new state constitutions of the era of the Revolution required ballot
papers. Kentucky clung to oral voting even after the Civil War,
otherwise the system had become general.[2]

The traditional method might persist in non-political circles.
As late as the 1880's, the by-laws of the Massachusetts Historical

[1] San Francisco *Alta California,* June 20, 1854; *The Public Papers of
David B. Hill,* 7 vols. (Albany, 1885–92), 1888, 112–13.

[2] Gosnell, "Ballot," 410; George Henry Moore, "Notes on Tything-men
and the Ballot in Massachusetts," *Proceedings of the American Antiquarian Society,* New Series, III (April, 1884), 81–91; Simeon E. Baldwin, "The Early History of the Ballot in Connecticut," *Papers of the
American Historical Association,* IV (October, 1890), 407–22; Spencer D.
Albright, *The American Ballot* (Washington, 1942), 14. Albright says
ballot papers were first used in America in 1629.

Society, guardian of the state's traditions, provided that elections follow the old colonial law of 1634—an ear of Indian corn to indicate a vote, and a bean a blank.[3]

The modern electoral system began in the 1820's when the courts in several key decisions accepted the use of printed ballots. The Electoral College described in the constitution was now a legal fiction; for the presidential election had become a contest between two political parties, and in most of the states the people directly elected the members of the College as a list of nonentities standing in for their party's national candidates. The franchise was becoming wider as state after state permitted full manhood suffrage. The same democratic and partisan spirit, especially in the new communities of the West, demanded the right to elect more and more officials at the three tiers of government. The political process inevitably became too complex for the average voter who was now expected to decide from among a host of candidates and propositions, and for the mechanical operation of this labor was expected to provide his own pen and paper as well. The parties were well entrenched, sustained by conflict and the growing pickings from salaries and disposal of the public bounty. What more natural than their managers should provide the elector with a ready-made slate of candidates? What more natural than they provide him with a printed ballot paper? And what more natural than they make the ballot paper recognizable from a distance and make sure that he used it?[4]

It has been shown how the disorderly conduct of elections in the United States had provided a weapon for opponents of Grote's valiant efforts to secure the ballot in Britain. American states did take steps to tinker with the system. Several states, beginning with Maine in 1831, passed laws prescribing the paper and ink to be

[3] Moore, "Notes on Tything-men and the Ballot in Massachusetts," 88. These officers had the onerous task of inspecting unlicensed houses and Sabbath-breaking.

[4] James Bryce, *The American Commonwealth* (1888), 2nd. ed., 2 vols. (New York, 1911), II, 146–55; *Henshaw v. Foster,* 9 Pickering (Mass.), 312, cit. Evans, *Australian Ballot System,* 2; *Hartington Committee,* Q. 10123–26.

used. New York secured with great difficulty a law in 1859 to register voters. "Ballot-stuffing" had become a fine art, especially in California, by concealing the papers under a false bottom of the box, or by surreptitiously folding tissue-ballots inside a larger paper. So strange new boxes were devised with glass sides and a bell and counting dial. But these were only palliatives and readily evaded, while the printed party ballot remained, in the words of the New York reformer, William Mills Ivins, as "the fatal gap in the law." As Charles Seymour and Donald Page Frary tersely put it, "unregulated political heelers were given virtually complete control of an essential part of the electoral system."[5]

Because of inadequate controls and partisan zeal, the electoral system was riddled with abuses: bribery, indirect bribery through official fees, intimidation, party assessments, "knifing," and repeating. These abuses had developed in American conditions and in response to local needs and values.

The simplest form of bribery occurred when ballot peddlers or district captains paid a voter as he emerged from the polling place. To check that he actually used the ballot it was colored or otherwise recognizable and the compliant voter was followed up to the box. The most notorious instance was a feature of the presidential election of 1888 in Indiana. The treasurer of the Republican national committee instructed his county chairmen as follows, thereby coining the phrase, "blocks of five," for permanent use: "Divide the floaters in blocks of five, and put a trusted man, with necessary funds, in charge of these five, and make them responsible that none get away." The main issue of that election was President Grover Cleveland's message in favor of tariff reform. The Democrats asserted that the Republican chairman, Matthew Quay of Pennsylvania, had soaked the protected manufacturers on an unprecedented scale and used the money to bring into or "colonize" the state of New York with temporary or subsidized lodgers. The word "floaters" in Indiana suggests the same practice, as bribery usually depended on other abuses such as repeating and personation. The

5 Ivins, *Machine Politics,* 76; L. E. Fredman, "The Bigler Regime," (Unpublished master's thesis, Stanford University, 1959), 44–45; Charles Seymour and Donald Page Frary, *How the World Votes: Democratic Development in Elections,* 2 vols. (Springfield, 1918), I, 248.

extent and acceptance of it became quite alarming. In 1892, the research of Professor J. J. McCook yielded the startling conclusion that sixteen percent of the voters of Connecticut were up for sale at prices ranging from two to twenty dollars. What is more, he found that three-fifths of a given sample were not shiftless lodgers or ignorant immigrants, but the descendants of virtuous Yankee yeomen.[6]

The use of a ballot box discouraged treating or bribery before election day, although the candidates frequently picked up the saloon bills. Another form of indirect bribery which flourished was more difficult to attack until Ivins delivered his famous addresses in February and March of 1887 entitled "Money in Elections." He showed the explicit and generous provision available for party workers on election day, partly from public funds and partly from assessments on the candidates.[7]

The older method of voting assumed that legitimate voters could be identified by their neighbors and officials at the polling place. However, it was rarely possible to identify the growing number of transients and city dwellers, and repeating and personation became only too easy. The New York registration law of 1859 led to some improvement in the conduct of elections and was copied elsewhere. Voters had to register in person and there was provision for ballot boxes and officials with definite powers. But a further loophole was soon apparent. For each of the eight hundred twelve electoral districts in the city, the Bureau of Elections chose four inspectors and two clerks, three from each party, who were paid at the generous rate of seven dollars and fifty cents a day. If a

[6] Robert LaFollette Jr., "The Adoption of the Australian Ballot in Indiana," *Indiana Magazine of History,* XXIV (June, 1928), 112–13; New York *Times,* October 23, November 1, 1888; J. J. McCook, "The Alarming Proportion of Venal Voters," *Forum,* XIV (September, 1892), 1–13; *The Nation,* LIV (May 19, 1892), 369. Indiana obtained a good Australian ballot law in 1889 which served as a model for the party column system.

[7] Ivins, *Machine Politics,* 39–44, 49, 56–57, 64. In Philadelphia in the 1880's, five thousand voters were paid to peddle the tickets. Charles Chauncey Binney, "The Australian Ballot System," *Lippincott's Monthly Magazine,* XLIV (September, 1889), 385–86. A witness told the Hartington Committee that elections in South Carolina in the 1850's were well conducted, but marred by some intimidation and much treating. *Hartington Committee,* Q. 10016ff.

23

federal office was on the ballot, two supervisors and two marshals were added to this patronage. Thus ten voters in each district were guaranteed and paid from the public funds. The assessments levied on candidates provided a pool sufficient to pay an average of forty-four ticket peddlers in each district at the ruling rate of five dollars. In all, fifty-four people in each district were under pay on election day, or twenty percent of the voters.[8]

By arranging the appointments, the leaders could reward the party workers on election day and retain their services. The leaders themselves usually held a full-time sinecure on the public payroll. A county clerk told a legislative committee which included the young Theodore Roosevelt that he was paid nearly eighty thousand dollars a year, from which he paid a clerk a small salary to do most of the work while he attended to the machine's business.[9]

The partisanship of these paid officials was sometimes ill-concealed. After the elections of November, 1889, in New Jersey, for example, the grand jury indicted sixty-seven officials. Undeterred, the machine reappointed most of them when released from prison. Though the boxes had a stamping mechanism, the officials had been supplied with tissue or "joker" ballots stamped elsewhere to use as required. The laws of many states still treat the election official as a partisan, and despite elaborate precautions produce similar consequences.[10]

Where paid peddlers were loitering outside the polling place there was bound to be some scuffling and intimidation. Sometimes the disorder was spontaneous and the result of partisan zeal; often it was deliberately contrived to frighten away decent people and magnify the coerced vote. Party meetings were often held in or adjacent to saloons for the same reason. Contemporaries also al-

[8] Ivins, *loc. cit.*; Joseph P. Harris, *Registration of Voters in the United States* (Washington, 1929), 72–78. The first registration law was passed in Massachusetts in 1800, but attracted little interest before the Civil War.

[9] Ivins, *loc. cit.*; Herman Hagedorn ed., *The Works of Theodore Roosevelt*, 20 vols. (New York, 1926), XIII, 85.

[10] Edward B. Grubb, "A Campaign for Ballot Reform," *North American Review*, CLV (December, 1892), 688–91. The author was the defeated Republican candidate who had made ballot reform a main issue of the election.

leged that workingmen were intimidated by manufacturers seeking their vote for protective tariffs or by agitators seeking their vote for Socialism.[11]

The worst and most disorderly elections occurred in the big cosmopolitan centers such as New York and San Francisco. Here the pickings and patronage were the greatest because there was a concentration of poor people and recent immigrants unused to the franchise. And here the rolls could easily be padded with fake names. The managers would naturalize non-existent aliens and en-roll non-existent lodgers from the flophouses. On election day, they would "colonize" or bring in hired repeaters to use the names. For example, in 1868, 41,112 aliens were naturalized in New York —84 in the month of January, 26,226 in October, and 24 in December—figures which speak for themselves. The *Nation* de-scribed how this was done:

> The naturalization mill has finished its work for this election, having ground out 35,000 voters in this city alone. Of these, 10,000 are perhaps rightly admitted, 10,000 having passed through the machine without having been here five years, and the other 15,000 have never, at any rate, been near the court room; indeed, from 5,000 to 7,000 of these latter are non-existent. . . . One of our upright judges . . . proceeded to call of a long string of purely imaginary names invented by him-self on the spur of the moment; John Smith, James Snooks, John Jones, Thomas Noakes, and the like. For every name, a man instantly answered and took a certificate!

In addition, both cities included a large proportion of Irish-born —to be precise, twenty-six percent of the population of New York in 1850. The clannish and rowdy Gael showed a ready talent for the art of winning office, and a menacing leer from a fire

---

[11] *Hartington Committee,* Q. 10063; W. M. Ivins, *Electoral Reform: the History of the Yates-Saxton Bill* (New York, 1888?), 10; Theodore Roosevelt, *An Autobiography* (New York, 1913), 63–64. On Protection, see New York *Times,* November 8, 1888. On intimidation by Labor, see *Century Illustrated Monthly Magazine,* XXXIII (March, 1887), 807; and Edward Wakefield, "The Australian Ballot System," *Forum,* VIII (Octo-ber, 1889), 156–58. The New Zealand law was passed in 1870. Wake-field, nephew of the noted colonial reformer, Edward Gibbon Wakefield, was then editor of the Wellington *Evening Press.*

The Australian Ballot:

company bravo secured many a vote. As peddlers and repeaters were often unsavory characters using unsavory methods, the political management of a large city encouraged crime in general.[12]

This is illustrated by the fierce intra-party faction which emerged in San Francisco during the Gold Rush. Within the Democratic party, "Tammany" and "Chivalry" battled for the rich patronage of the new state and her seats in the United States Senate, and were, despite the names, only marginally concerned with the complexities of sectional politics. The rival leaders were David C. Broderick who had learned his trade as a fireman and Locofoco ward boss in New York, and William McKendree Gwin who had learned his on the stump in Tennessee and who served for most of the 1850's in the Senate. Broderick coveted the post with obsessive zeal and his bid dominated the business of four sessions of the state legislature. The polling places in San Francisco were manned by his cohorts, known as the "bhoys" or the "shoulder-strikers," accomplished in the arts of scuffling and ballot-stuffing. As tissue ballots required some sleight of hand, they often supplied boxes with a sliding, false bottom which concealed the spare votes. In June, 1854, the Tammany faction prepared to capture San Francisco for the party's state convention. A reporter seemed fascinated as he described the unsurpassed violence:

> Some of the prominent actors in these outrageous proceedings behaved like maniacs let loose from Bedlam. As the day drew to a close, wild riot came on apace on the wings of the evening, black eyes and bloody noses abounded. These were trifles of too little interest to slake the thirst that seemed to rage for

[12] Florence Gibson, *The Attitudes of the New York Irish towards State and National Affairs: 1848–92* (New York, 1951), 79, 81, 227; *The Nation,* VII (October 29, 1868), 341; A. C. Bernheim, "The Ballot in New York," *Political Science Quarterly,* IV (March, 1889), 135; Ivins, *Electoral Reform,* 24–26; Fredman, "The Bigler Regime," 38–71. For a scathing opinion of the Irish Democrats in the legislature of 1882, see Elting E. Morison ed., *The Letters of Theodore Roosevelt,* 8 vols. (Cambridge, 1951–54), II, 470. For Torrens' opinion of the Irish in Australia, see *Hartington Committee,* Q. 8728–35. For evidence of fraud in New York, see New York *Times,* March 29, 1888, and City Reform Club material in the Welling Papers (New York Public Library, Manuscript Division).

more exciting incidents. Knives were drawn and freely used, revolvers discharged with a perfect recklessness. . . . The police had they interfered would have stood a chance of being annihilated.

The editor dismissed the proceedings as a farce, but the city had a Tammany delegation. The rest of the story may be summarized briefly. The murder of the crusading editor, James King of William, led to a fierce outcry against "the murderers and ballot-box stuffers," and the setting up of the second Vigilance Committee of 1856. Broderick quickly left the city. In September, 1859, now Senator at last, he lost his life in a duel and fortunately for his reputation was soon regarded as a martyr and victim of the Slavocracy.[13]

Another abuse was the practice of assessing candidates, ostensibly to pay for the ballots and their distribution. As Ivins disclosed, the receipts were enormous, providing a generous pool for the peddlers or paid voters and largely confining candidates to the rich men who could afford such a sum. Of course others might borrow and expect to recoup the debt when in office— William Marcy Tweed and David C. Broderick followed a fairly well-traveled road from a fire company to a legislature. Ivins devised this table which revealed the amount of assessments, probably for the first time in print. It was an estimate of the amounts levied in an average year in New York City assuming two candidates in each electoral district:

Two aldermanic candidates at $15 each for 812 districts	$24,360
Two assembly candidates at $10 each for 812 districts	16,240
Two congressional candidates at $25 each for 812 districts	40,600
Four judicial candidates at $10,000 each	40,000
Two mayoral candidates at $20,000 each	40,000
Two county candidates, say for sheriff, at $10,000 each	20,000
Two candidates for comptroller at $10,000 each	20,000
Two candidates for district attorney at $5,000 each	10,000
	$211,000

[13] San Francisco *Alta California,* June 20, 1854, July 26, 1853 ("Song of the Shoulder-strikers"), and May 15–16, 1856.

The Australian Ballot:

The total costs of elections in New York in the 1880's could roughly be rendered as follows:

Providing tickets	$203,000	paid by the candidates.
Rent of rooms, etc.	$200,000	paid from donations and party funds.
Officials under the law	$290,000	paid from public funds.

So that elections in one year cost about seven hundred thousand dollars, to which should be added a large portion of the one million dollars for the salaries of politicians on the public payroll.[14]

As the ballot was printed and distributed by the party boss, there was no safe guarantee that he would not "knife" or trade off a candidate in return for the opposition supporting another part of the ticket. It was generally believed that in New York the upstate Republicans and Tammany Hall, the Democratic party machine in the city, had had some such arrangement since the days of William Seward and Thurlow Weed. The form of the ballot paper permitted this. They were often called "tickets" because they consisted of a long list of names like a railroad ticket. The list for each area contained a different combination of the national, state and local offices, which the party might print especially for the area or might bunch together as required. It was therefore not difficult to remove or alter names of candidates on the list whom the bosses disliked or had arranged to knife. A person bribed could say yea or nay; but knifing was outright deception of the voter. Every time there was a big discrepancy between candidates on one ticket, the charge was made. Sometimes it seems indisputable.[15]

Although American electors frequently crossed party lines, the very possibility of knifing led to endless suspicions. A noted instance occurred during the presidential elections of 1888. The incumbent, Grover Cleveland of upstate New York, was running against the Republican Benjamin Harrison. In his home state, Governor David B. Hill, also from upstate, was rapidly

14 Ivins, *Machine Politics*, 56–57, 63–64.
15 Binney, "The Australian Ballot System," 387–88.

emerging as an accomplished Democratic state boss with national aspirations. In the national canvas, Cleveland defeated Harrison by a small plurality, but lost in New York and accordingly lost in the Electoral College—the reverse of his hectic fight with James G. Blaine in 1884 when he had narrowly taken New York. Harrison's plurality in the state was 12,787; but Hill, also running for re-election, gained a plurality of 17,740 over the Republican candidate for governor. In the city he ran about eleven thousand votes ahead of Cleveland's plurality. In addition, Tammany candidates won the city offices and fifteen of the city's twenty-four assembly districts. Because of the discrepancy, the nonpartisan reformers and leaders of the rival County Democracy charged Hill and Tammany with betraying the national ticket. "A better man never was sacrificed to a meaner one," thundered the New York *Times.* They alleged that in the eighth district, for example, Republican peddlers had been distributing Tammany's congressional and county tickets. By his veto of liquor and ballot-reform bills and by "trading" part of the ticket, they alleged that Hill had co-operated with Tammany to ensure his re-election at Cleveland's expense. An even hotter fight for ballot reform seemed likely in the next session of the New York legislature. Combined with "blocks of five" in Indiana and charges of Protectionist bribery, the circumstances of the election of 1888 gave a surging push to a movement whose legislative achievement to date was simply a local law for Louisville, Kentucky, and the model law of Massachusetts.[16]

[16] New York *Times,* November 8, 1888; *Harper's Weekly,* November 10, 1888; Bernheim, "The Ballot in New York," 136; Herbert J. Bass, *I am a Democrat: the Political Career of David Bennett Hill* (Syracuse, 1961), 122–25; George F. Parker, *Recollections of Grover Cleveland* (New York, 1911), 342–43. The *Times* and *Harper's,* whose editor was George Curtis, president of the National Civil Service Reform League, supported a split ticket including Cleveland and excluding Hill. Bass argues convincingly that Hill did not knife Cleveland—he would have avoided the strife of 1892 if Cleveland had won in 1888 and served a second term. Cleveland himself told Parker that the national issues (tariff) and local issues (liquor reform) were quite separate, and many voters

The Australian Ballot:

Despite the various abuses of elections, there was a fundamental safeguard. The bosses and ward heelers and special interests who exploited the process could not operate in a completely arbitrary and despotic manner. The nation accepted the ideal of a popular and democratic government, and at least the formalities of an election had to be observed. The ballot box was thus a potent symbol.

The fierce outcry against ballot box stuffing in California in the 1850's has already been mentioned. It was assumed by the press that this was a grave accusation and typified the corruption and misgovernment of the era. Throughout 1871, Thomas Nast, cartoonist for *Harper's Weekly,* had been lampooning the simian-looking spoilsmen and repeaters used by the Tweed Ring in New York City. As the state and local elections approached, he produced one of the most famous cartoons in the history of American journalism. The press and reformers had been gathering proof of the Ring's theft and corruption—Nast's cartoon now had the fierceness, the directness and clear symbols which could turn a movement into a crusade. The issue bore the date of November 11, 1871. In a Roman arena, the Tammany tiger lay athwart the fair and defiled body of the Republic, while the caption announced simply: "What are you going to do about it?" The tiger was the emblem of the Americus or Big Six Fire Company, Tweed's first vehicle for political power. The significant symbolism in the cartoon included not only the tiger and the fair maiden, but also a shattered ballot box. When Nast celebrated victory three weeks later, he depicted a large ballot box in the foreground as the weapon of an aroused people.[17]

By this time, many people were aware that American elections were riddled with abuses. It was a more difficult problem

---

would have split their tickets. Even so, there was growing animosity between the two men. The charge could be made and readily believed. In 1892, Hill engineered a "snap" state convention to secure the delegates. In 1894, as a United States Senator, he blocked Cleveland's New York nominee for the Supreme Court.

[17] *Harper's Weekly,* November 11, December 2, 1871.

to tackle than in Britain because of the vested interests and
the greater complexity of the American political system. The
early critics had no specific plans. For example in 1880, George
W. Julian asserted: "The inquiry is daily becoming more pertinent whether elections any longer elect." The writer had com-
pleted a political circle as a Free-soil Democrat, Republican,
Liberal, and supporter of Tilden in 1876, and was now a sort
of professional reformer living in Indianapolis. His greatest
work on land reform lay ahead. Julian's "remedy" for the
abuses of elections consisted of the windy rhetoric of "more
popular government" and "faith." Within a decade, the Australian ballot was to be canvased and adopted as such a remedy.[18]

The first Australian ballot law in the United States was an
act passed in February, 1888, to amend the charter of Louisville,
Kentucky, and confined to elections in that city. Paradoxically,
Kentucky was the last state to abandon oral voting. The law
was drafted by Arthur Wallace and passed by the predomi-
nantly Democratic legislature of which he was a member with
only one dissent. The law seems to have been modeled on the
British statute, but had some interesting features of its own.
It provided for an official, blanket ballot supplied at the city's
expense; candidates were nominated by a petition filed with the
fee of twenty dollars ten days before the election; their names
were arranged alphabetically under the office with provision
for write-in candidates; the ballots were bound in a book with
numbered stubs for taking the voters' names; the voter marked
by a cross, or signified yes or no to a proposition, and placed his
ballot in an envelope; a compartment was provided for every
one hundred seventy-five voters and the physical arrangements
were carefully described; the clerk could assist incapacitated
persons and endorsed the stub accordingly; and finally, several
clauses defined and penalized corrupt practices. About twelve
months later, while the citizens of Massachusetts were awaiting
a test of their new Australian ballot law, a citizen of Louisville

[18] George W. Julian, "The Abuse of the Ballot and its Remedy," *International Review,* VIII (May, 1880), 534–45.

advised them that the law was easily administered and had checked the corruption once very noticeable in his city.[19]

In 1889, the system was extended to the more populous counties and cities of the state and then gradually enlarged. People were soon quarreling about the authorship of the law. Louis N. Dembitz claimed that he had read an outline modeled on the British law to a club in Louisville in October, 1887, while Wallace replied that it was properly known as the Wallace law, and drafted by several people encouraged by Henry George's article in the *North American Review* of March, 1883.[20]

When John Wigmore asked whether the American people had their Dutton or Nicholson, he could have mentioned George. For the noted reformer and author of *Progress and Poverty* (1879), one of the most influential works of the century, was also one of the pioneers of the Australian ballot in the United States. He was the first to advocate it in print. In December, 1871, when a California editor and an active Democrat, George anticipated most of the arguments later put forward in the United States in an article in the *Overland Monthly*. He pointed out that a public ballot removed the excuse for party assessments; a truly secret vote made bribery a risk; and a blanket ballot gave partisan and independent candidates an equal chance. In addition, George acutely suggested that the "motor" of the present evils was a slack public opinion, and that mere reform was not sufficient. He made the suggestion, which was not entirely facetious, that since the candidates and bosses calculated what the election cost and what the offices would yield them, it would be simpler to auction the offices and pay the proceeds to the Treasury.[21]

[19] Wigmore, *Australian Ballot System*, 24–26, 138–43. Boston *Daily Advertiser*, January 11, 1889.

[20] *The Nation*, LIV (January 14, 1892), 32, (February 4, 1892), 87.

[21] John H. Wigmore, "A Summary of Ballot Reform," *The Nation*, XLIX (August 29, 1889), 165; Henry George, "Bribery in Elections," *Overland Monthly*, VII (December, 1871), 497–504. He referred to the Australian ballot at page 500. The sly reference to the Chinese at the end is typical of California at this time.

Song of the Shoulder-Striker

A provocative article entitled "Money in Elections" opened the issue of the *North American Review* for March, 1883, and produced the aforementioned result in Kentucky. The great expense of elections gave the people who furnished the money special privileges, George argued. He urged the adoption of the Australian ballot as "the greatest single reform." The time was ripe in the year of the Pendleton Act, which created a classified civil service based on merit. The owner-editor of the *Review*, Allen Thorndike Rice, had built up an influential journal in which George frequently appeared, along with E. L. Godkin, David Wells and other prominent reformers. Rice too became an eager champion of the Australian ballot.[22]

Thereafter George was persistent. As a result of his effective and well-supported campaign for mayor of New York in 1886, a United Labor party was formed. Although almost invisible at the presidential elections of 1888, they were the first national party to demand the reform in their platform, and indeed the only party to do so before it had swept the country. The relevant section read:

> Since the ballot is the only means by which in our republic the redress of political and social grievances is to be sought, we especially and emphatically declare for the adoption of what is known as the Australian system of voting, in order that the effectual secrecy of the ballot, and the relief of candidates for public office from the heavy expenses now imposed upon them, may prevent bribery and intimidation, do away with practical discriminations in favour of the rich and unscrupulous, and lessen the pernicious influence of money in politics.

Later it will be shown that labor and trade union groups actively supported the reform in various cities and states. George advocated it in the *Standard*, which he ran as a weekly in New York between January, 1887, and August, 1892. Several feature articles in May and June, 1888, supported the ballot bill then before the New York legislature. He described it as "the one

[22] Henry George, "Money in Elections," *North American Review*, CXXXVI (March, 1883), 201–11; Editorial, "Recent Reforms in Balloting," *ibid.*, CXLII (December, 1886), 628–42.

primary reform that will make easier all other reforms." But generally, the paper was a vehicle for the owner and his self-appointed destiny as the Savonarola of the Single-tax, and his claimed circulation of twenty thousand is probably exaggerated.[23]

During his brief tour of Australia, George addressed a large public meeting in the Sydney town hall on March 6, 1890, on the subject of "The Land and the People." The advance interview, the mayor in the chair, and the report of five-and-a-half columns indicated the regard in which he was held in the antipodes, a regard not lessened by his brief reference to the Australian ballot. George mentioned his article of 1883 and the adoption of the reform in several American states. "If you can teach us more, for God's sake teach it—advance Australia," he declared to thunderous applause. Finally, George was listed in a circular of 1896 with other prominent reformers as a vice-president of the New York Ballot Reform League.[24]

[23] *Appleton's Annual Encyclopaedia and Register of Important Events for the Year 1888* (New York, 1889), 773–80; John J. Ingalls, "A Fair Vote and an Honest Count," in John D. Long ed., *The Republican Party: its History, Principles, and Policies* (New York, 1888); New York *Standard*, May 12, 1888 in Henry George Papers (New York Public Library, Economics Division). The United Labor party received only 2,818 votes at the elections of 1888. The Republican platform included "effective legislation to secure the integrity and purity of elections which are the fountains of all public authority"; however, Ingalls in the campaign book concentrated on the intimidation of southern Republicans.

[24] Sydney *Daily Telegraph*, March 6–7, 1890. George had touched at Melbourne in 1855 as a sixteen-year-old foremast boy, and his wife was Australian born. George's papers shed some light on an interesting and related question—How did these professional reformers of the late-nineteenth century live? His lecture fee was one hundred dollars, strangely too high for a group of middle-class reformers. George Iles to R. R. Bowker, September 25, 1889, Society for Political Education Letterbook, Bowker Papers (New York Public Library, Manuscript Division). The quality periodicals paid about three-quarters of a cent a word, so the usual ten-page article in the *North American Review* would yield about twenty-five dollars. Frank Luther Mott, *A History of American Magazines*, 4 vols. (New York, 1930–57), *passim*. Chance references in other sources bear out these figures for articles and lectures. Dr. Charles A. Barker, author of the standard biography of George, kindly commented on September 5, 1962. His impression is that George relied mainly on gifts and journalism, was careless with money, and spent much on traveling for the cause.

Song of the Shoulder-Striker

If George was the Dutton or Nicholson, the American Chapman was perhaps George Walthew of Detroit. In 1885, Walthew, a twenty-five-year-old lawyer recently elected to the Michigan legislature on the Democratic and Greenback ticket, introduced a bill based on the Canadian Australian ballot law. It was soundly defeated in a house evenly balanced between the parties. Two years later, a revised bill presented by Judson Grenell of Detroit passed the lower house but lapsed in the Senate. Grenell was connected with the Knights of Labor and the labor press, and had been nominated by the Independent Labor party. By 1889, there was a widespread demand for the reform and the bill promoted by Edwin Fox, Republican, passed by a large majority. The reformers were dissatisfied with the act; and according to Arthur C. Ludington's digest of *American Ballot Laws: 1888–1910,* Michigan's first Australian ballot law was passed in the session of 1891.[25]

The Detroit *Free Press,* which had the largest circulation in the state, praised the aims of Walthew's bill, but claimed it would be too cumbersome for a voter to choose from two hundred candidates. The editorial might well have drawn attention to the story of intimidation and fraudulent counting in the local elections on the very next page.[26]

Another early advocate was Robert Schilling, one of those little-known and strenuous reformers who was a leader of the Coopers' Union and of the Greenback party in Cleveland, and later of the Knights of Labor and the Populist party in Milwaukee. In 1891, he became widely known as the first national secretary of the Populist party. An article in the *Labor Advance* in December, 1877, which he edited in the Greenback interest in Cleveland, urged certain changes which later reformers assumed as part of the Australian ballot. Like George, Schilling was not a Socialist; rather, both men expressed that constant opposition to monopoly which was heard in various guises from Jackson to Wilson. With his extensive interests, his unremitting public speaking, journalism

[25] Wigmore, *Australian Ballot System,* 23–24; Arthur C. Ludington, *American Ballot Laws, 1888–1910,* Education Department Bulletin Number 488 (Albany, 1911), 36; Detroit *Free Press,* January 27, April 22, 1885, June 29, 1889.
[26] Detroit *Free Press,* January 27, 1885.

35

and party intrigues, it is unlikely that he could have found the time to develop what was no more than a casual suggestion in favor of ballot reform.[27]

Although these people were aware of the abuses to be remedied and a specific reform to remedy them, they had yet to draft a practical law for American conditions. Indeed, the Oxford-educated Allen Thorndike Rice in his article of December, 1886, assumed a parallel between British and American elections. The model bill which he drafted and which was adopted by George and the United Labor party had some most peculiar features. The nominations were received at the registration of voters and a candidate was placed on the ballot once he had obtained a call from one-tenth of the voters last registered. There was also a separate ballot paper for each office. The system assumed that only one or a few offices were being filled at an election and was unlikely to work in the United States. The press criticism of the Walthew bill, which also required separate ballots, was justifiable. America's Chapman would have to find a place in his new system for the party ticket and party loyalties.[28]

The reformer responsible for the first state-wide Australian ballot law was a different type. Richard Henry Dana III was an arch-Mugwump who belonged to one of the most distinguished families of Massachusetts. Both his father and grandfather followed a career embracing law, politics and literature, and the former (1815–82) had won fame as the author of the minor classic, *Two Years before the Mast,* and as a noted authority on international law. Highly conscious of his background, the young Richard followed a similar career and made an appropriate marriage with the daughter of Henry Wadsworth Longfellow. Like Theodore Roosevelt and Richard Welling, two other active reformers, he became a noted sportsman at Harvard and captain of rowing. Such a man was near the center of the close-knit social

[27] Milton M. Small, "The Biography of Robert Schilling," (Unpublished master's thesis, University of Wisconsin, 1953), 33–34, 104fn., 159–60.

[28] Editorial, "Recent Reforms in Balloting," *North American Review,* CXLII (December, 1886), 628–42; James Redpath, "Electoral Reform," *ibid.,* CXLV (October, 1887), 451–54.

and intellectual elite of the Boston-Cambridge area, and his many correspondents in public life included presidents Roosevelt and Cleveland.[29]

In his study and practice of international law, Dana's father had made friends with an English authority, William Vernon Harcourt, later a Liberal member of parliament and minister. Harcourt entertained the young son in England and wrote to him occasionally. In 1886, he asked the thirty-five-year-old Boston lawyer why few able and idealistic men entered politics in the United States. Dana recalled that like most people he blamed it on the elections, and was increasingly disturbed as he tried to explain this to Harcourt's satisfaction.[30]

Conditions in Massachusetts on election days were as bad as elsewhere. In 1851, a law backed by the Democrats and Free-soilers was passed requiring that ballots be placed in official envelopes provided. The Whigs killed the reform in 1853, unsatis-

---

[29] Bliss Perry, *Richard Henry Dana, 1851–1931* (Boston, 1933), John P. Marquand, *The Late George Apley* (Boston, 1937), Arthur Mann, *Yankee Reformers in the Urban Age* (Cambridge, 1954), 236–37; Van Wyck Brooks, *New England: Indian Summer, 1865–1915* (New York, 1940), 425–26. A further attempt will be made to examine the Mugwump type in Chapter VI. While Dana resembled the subject of Marquand's novel, it is most unfair of Brooks to describe him as a man of inferior capacity, tormented by the demands of family tradition and the typical disease of "grandfather on the brain." My impression, gathered from Perry's biography and the Dana Papers (Massachusetts Historical Society) is that he was a sensible and productive individual. Dr. Mann's attitude to the older families is similar; they are ignored, or typified by Henry Adams in his most pessimistic moods. There is no discussion of the Australian ballot or similar reforms. He concentrates on Benjamin Flower and the contributors to his periodical, *The Arena* (1889–96), who were mainly concerned with Edward Bellamy's Nationalism, the social gospel, and the settlement house movement. Dr. Mann's aims stated in his Preface are to demonstrate Boston's reform spirit after the age of Emerson; to show the beginnings of modern liberalism in the city as well as on the farm; and to relate reform to the characteristics of a particular community. The treatment is surely too narrow.

[30] Dana, "Sir William Vernon Harcourt and the Australian Ballot Law," *Proceedings of the Massachusetts Historical Society,* LVIII (June, 1925), 401–05. Harcourt's interest in Boston was enhanced by his second marriage in 1876 to the daughter of the noted historian, John L. Motley.

factory as it was, by making it optional. The need and effectiveness of a secret ballot was forcibly demonstrated two years later when Charles Sumner was proposed for the Senate of the United States. There were twenty-five fruitless ballots, and in some the number cast exceeded the number of members—the legislators could stuff ballots too. Finally, they agreed to place each in a sealed envelope and Sumner was duly elected on the twenty-sixth, when the ballots were equal to the number of legislators voting. By the 1880's, the use of boxes with a counting device had eliminated stuffing and outright fraud; but the parties continued to distribute their ballots for the many offices under contest, and practiced bribery and intimidation to make sure that they were used.[31]

Dana was already known as a reformer and draftsman of the Massachusetts civil service law of 1883. He raised the matter before a small dining club of reformers called the Dutch Treat, whose members after a discussion asked him to report on an official, blanket and secret ballot. Some, following John Stuart Mill, preferred open voting as a principle; but they were persuaded as Forster had been to accept the practical benefits of the new scheme. The group compared papers arranged by office block and party column. They felt that as the latter was speedier, it would disclose an independent or nonpartisan voter. This was a real problem for a man like Dana, a nominal Republican who supported Cleveland in 1884 and 1888.

When the Massachusetts legislature assembled for the session of 1888, it had before it nineteen petitions for electoral reform from the Common Council of Boston, and various township, labor, and reform groups. A bill was introduced into the Senate and referred to the committee on electoral laws chaired by Henry Sprague, a member of the Dutch Treat club. When the hearings began on February 12, Dana learned for the first time of the Australian ballot law, "which we had invented afresh." He put in evidence another letter from Harcourt on the operation of the British law. The committee also received a bill drafted by Charles

31 *Ibid.*; Wigmore, *Australian Ballot System,* 29; Vote by Ballot Society, *Tracts on the Ballot; Number Five* (London, 1855).

Saxton, a member of the New York legislature, which Sprague requested Dana to use in re-drafting his own bill for presentation to the Senate. Under Sprague's guidance, the bill passed the Senate by eighteen votes to ten, and the lower house by one hundred twenty-one to forty-one. It bore the date, May 29, 1888.[32]

Dana did not consider his task done by merely drafting the law. He became treasurer of the Ballot Act League established in June, 1889, to prepare for the first elections under it. He lectured with sample booths and ballot papers and wrote letters to the press explaining the new system. He appeared before legislative committees in his own and other states. His papers also contain a detailed and measured pencil sketch of a polling place, endorsed—"designed and drawn by R. H. Dana, 1888"—and a draft of a four-page pamphlet entitled *The Voters Duties under the New Ballot Act of Massachusetts.*[33]

The Massachusetts law was first tested in the elections of November, 1889, and was an undoubted success. It was generally agreed that the voting was fair and orderly, and there were more and better candidates. The cost to the state was small—$8,175 to print one million ballot papers, and thirty-five dollars for the fittings of each precinct, which were portable and re-usable. The average time taken to complete the supposedly complex ballot was only two minutes. Dana argued that the voter turnout was high, compared with other non-presidential years, and the voters did not neglect candidates well down the ballot paper. The careful drafting and successful application of this law made it a model for many reformers elsewhere. As for Massachusetts, the Boston

[32] Dana, "Sir William Vernon Harcourt and the Australian Ballot Law," 410; Dana, "The Practical Working of the Australian System of Voting in Massachusetts," 733–50; Massachusetts, *Journal of the House of Representatives,* and *Journal of the Senate* (Boston, 1888), *passim.* Dana said the agitation was begun a year-and-a-half before that in New York, but was imprecise about dates. He also repeated his objections to the party column system. Dana, "The Practical Working of the Australian System of Voting in Massachusetts," 733, 736.

[33] This material and a copy of the Saxton bill with his notations in pencil can be found in a folder marked "Australian Ballot." Dana Papers. Dana was at this time also the editor of the *Civil Service Record.*

Daily Advertiser acknowledged the first trial by declaring that "the whole system of our politics is likely to be changed." Attention steadily shifted to other reforms proposed by such earnest, intelligent and untypical voters as Dana.[34]

Scarcely less important than Dana was John Henry Wigmore, author of *The Australian Ballot System as Embodied in the Legislation of Various Countries,* which was published in two editions in 1889, and is the only contemporary book on the subject. Wigmore is known throughout the entire Common Law world for his standard *Treatise on Evidence,* and was connected with the Northwestern University Law School for fifty years until his death in 1943. Born and reared in San Francisco, he was at the time of writing a twenty-six-year-old graduate of Harvard and a member of the Boston bar. The historical introduction dealt with Australia, Britain, and then tersely with Massachusetts and the twenty-six other states or territories where the matter had been dealt with. There followed in full or summary form the laws in various countries, notes on their practical application, and a digest of legal decisions. In the preface to his second edition, the young reformer urged people in every state to send him a copy of any bill presented to their legislature, plus an account of the history of the agitation.[35]

As Dana had indicated, the movement in New York was quite independent of that in Boston. The burgeoning metropolis at the mouth of the Hudson River absorbed the teeming masses from Europe and much of the corporate wealth of the nation. The abuses of elections and the vested interests which profited thereby

[34] Boston *Daily Advertiser,* April 28, 1888, November 6, 1889; Dana, "The Practical Working of the Australian System of Voting in Massachusetts," 738–47; *Public Opinion,* November 16, 1889 (seventeen papers quoted); Adelbert Ames, "The New Method of Voting," *North American Review,* CXLIX (December, 1889), 752–54.

[35] William R. Roalfe, "John Henry Wigmore: Scholar and Reformer," *Journal of Criminal Law, Criminology and Police Science,* LIII (September, 1962), 277–300. With the energy typical of such men, Wigmore produced a third, ten-volume edition of his *Treatise* in 1940, at the age of seventy-seven. This work is the crowning product of the digest technique, which he utilized in a small way in his book on the Australian ballot.

appeared at their worst, and reformers were compelled to use the utmost vigor and persistence. Their clubs provided the intellectual stimulus and concerted action which were essential to promote the Australian ballot and other major reforms in the United States.

Most of the members were busy lawyers, journalists and independent businessmen who appreciated a monthly dinner-meeting where they could enjoy the food and company, and ponder one of the issues of the day. In the papers of the editor and publisher Richard Rogers Bowker are the invitations to three meetings of the recently established Commonwealth Club, held on February 28, March 15, and April 2, 1887. The speaker was William Mills Ivins, and his topics were: "The Purchase of Nominations and the Use of Money in Elections"; "The Remedy for Bribery and Corruption at Elections"; and "The Feasibility of Printing and Distributing Ballots at the Government's Expense." Born in New York and a graduate of Columbia Law School, the thirty-six-year-old Ivins had been elected Chamberlain in 1885 on the County Democratic ticket. (Bowker was a Republican and a bolter in 1884, but the members' only commitment was to civil service reform.) With unique detail and sense of purpose, Ivins gave specific information on the "fatal gap in the law" which made party ballots, bosses, and such costly and disorderly elections necessary. There were certain remedies suggested by the British example and "naturally suggested by the evil." If the ballots were printed and distributed at the public expense, there would be no need for an organization to provide ballots and candidates and levy tribute for their cost. The best candidates could come forward, and it should then be feasible to strictly limit the campaign expenditures and to disfranchise electors under pay. The New York *Evening Post,* edited by E. L. Godkin, and its sister-weekly, the *Nation,* the main organs of Mugwump opinion, responded immediately. Later in the year, the firm of Harpers added an earlier article by Ivins to his addresses and published a book of five substantial chapters.[36]

[36] Ivins, *Machine Politics,* 76, 86–87; *The Nation,* XLIV (March 3,

The Australian Ballot:

In October, the club appointed a committee which included Bowker to draft a bill and press for its passage. The City Reform Club took one hundred copies of Ivins' book and appointed representatives to this committee. Endorsed by several of the citizen clubs and the United Labor party, this bill came before the legislature in the session of 1888 as the Yates bill. Another was produced by Charles Saxton, a Republican assemblyman from Clyde. The bill which finally emerged from the judiciary committee bore both names and passed both houses on party lines. The Assembly divided by sixty-five Republicans and ten Democrats in favor, and one Republican and thirty-five Democrats against; and the Senate by eighteen Republicans and two Democrats in favor, and eight Democrats against.[37]

As the Democratic machine was opposed to the bill, there were further obstacles to be overcome. Tammany Hall ran the machine in the city and worked closely with the governor, an upstate Democrat, David Bennett Hill of Elmira, who made party loyalty his faith and slogan. Working steadily to replace Grover Cleveland as candidate and favorite son, he was determined to make no commitment or gesture, as Cleveland had done, to the groups in both parties seeking civil service or ballot reform. The aqueduct scandal, which broke early in the session, drove Hill and Tammany Hall closer together. The governor had repaid a political obligation in the city by accepting a high bid which permitted his creditor to sub-contract for a large profit. In addition,

1887), 180, (March 10, 1887), 204, (March 17, 1887), 222–23. In 1905 Ivins stood unsuccessfully for mayor as a Republican candidate against William Randolph Hearst and George B. McClellan. Henry Villard, who had financed the purchase of the *Evening Post* in 1881, and E. L. Godkin were also members of the Commonwealth Club.

[37] Ivins, *Electoral Reform, passim;* New York *Times,* March 31, May 3, 10, 18, 1888. The draft bill and other material are in the Bowker Papers. See also City Reform Club minutes, Welling Papers (New York Public Library, Manuscript Division). Richard Welling, like a number of people, belonged to both clubs and in 1890 was treasurer of both. The club draft had an office block arrangement, but the bill provided a party column. The solitary Republican negative vote in the Assembly was cast by the state boss, Thomas Collier Platt.

his veto of the excise bill greatly pleased the brewing interests.[38]

Hill still had thirty days after the legislature rose on May 11 in which to review bills. He waited a fortnight and then conducted a hearing, at which two Tammany lawyers opposed the bill, and Saxton and George spoke in favor. Many people claimed that he was delaying the veto to bargain for re-nomination. Whatever the cause, he waited almost until the deadline and then issued a veto message dated June 9, 1888.[39]

The arguments are interesting and deserve a brief summary. They range from the pertinent to the patently ridiculous. He described a ballot as a paper containing only the names of those voted for. It was every man's right to nominate and discuss his candidate at any time. Accordingly, the bill was harmful because of the wide powers of the election officials, the gap between nominations and election day, and the use of an exclusive or official ballot containing all the candidates. In addition, the illiterate voter was mocked and hindered in exercising his fundamental rights. In a glowing passage, Governor Hill reminded the Irish ward heelers that perfidious Albion herself had devised this sinister design upon his right of "discussion," and challenged such an unpatriotic and reactionary assault inspired from without. He said:

> The system contemplated by this bill is a mongrel one, which has not been tested anywhere by experience. . . . Here the people are upon an equality, and at the ballot-box all are freemen and equals. It has never heretofore been regarded as a crime for one citizen peaceably to discuss with his neighbour at the polls the merits of the various parties and candidates,

[38]W. M. Ivins to Daniel S. Lamont, July 25, 1888, Cleveland Papers (Library of Congress) ; Ivins, *Electoral Reform,* 61–62. In 1896, the reformers who had spurned Hill for a decade were now supporting him as a Gold Democrat. He opened his speech to the national convention in his customary way—"I am a Democrat, but I am not a revolutionist." New Orleans *Daily Picayune,* July 10, 1896.

[39] New York *Times,* May 26, June 7, 1888. The reformers asserted the city boses were also responsible for the omission of electoral and civil service reform from the recent Democratic national platform. For a scathing comment from the young Republican, Theodore Roosevelt, see his New York speech of December 13, 1888. Hagedorn ed., *Works of Theodore Roosevelt,* XIV, 81–87.

and to compare views and to inform each other, if they desired, how they intended to vote. . . . I realize that there is a class of well-meaning people who seem to hail with delight every new scheme which masquerades under the seductive name of 'reform,' especially if it comes from foreign shores and bears the approval of a monarchial government.[40]

The likelihood that Hill had knifed Cleveland in New York, the vast expenditures attributed to the Republican party boss, Matthew Quay, and the presentation of Australian ballot bills in many other states, spurred the reformers to even greater efforts in the session of 1889. Saxton again led the attack in the Assembly, and emphasized the abuses of the last elections. He criticized the Democratic bills for omitting an exclusive, blanket ballot, which provided an excuse for retaining party assessments and the opportunity for knifing other candidates on the ticket.[41]

The governor also discussed the recent elections in his annual message; but keeping within the terms of the party platform, blamed the protected manufacturers and their huge gifts to the Republican party. He urged piecemeal reforms, such as booths to ensure secrecy, but still refused to accept an exclusive, blanket ballot. He repeated all his old arguments in an expected veto message dated May 13, thirty pages in length. He included his most petty objections—what if the ballots were not delivered, or a nominee died?—and assumed a conservative role as he chided the legislature for their "mad anxiety" and "reckless haste."[42]

[40] *Public Papers of David B. Hill,* 1888, 112–13; New York *Times,* June 12–13, 1888. Hill's argument is riddled with inconsistencies. Printed party ballots obviously produced the same "gap." To say the voter could then "scratch" and write in his last-minute choice was contrary to Hill's definition of a ballot. He said that in Australia candidates still paid the expenses of the election; but the word "deposit" was there used in its literal sense, as it is today.

[41] New York *Times,* November 1, 7–8, 1888, April 10, 1889; Wigmore, *Australian Ballot System,* 26–27. The *Times* described the Democratic bills as fakes, provided by "their party's evil genius, David B. Hill."

[42] *Public Papers of David B. Hill,* 1889, 12–20, 144–74; New York *Times,* May 13, 1889. He proposed a legal two-hour break on election day to aid workingmen, as in the Massachusetts law. Australian elections then as now are held on a Saturday. There was an interesting but brief reference to the simpler form of elections under the British parliamentary system. *Ibid.,* 161–62.

Song of the Shoulder-Striker

In private, Hill was quite frank about his partisan aims. "I want a bill that is right," he wrote, "and that will protect our voters, or else I do not want any at all." His private secretary, Timothy Shaler Williams, was asked to write to an active Boston Democrat after the trial there and received some alarming news. There was no provision for illiterates and the office block arrangement had encouraged splitting of the ticket and neglect of the lower offices. The writer added:

> It has worked, I think, as we expected it would—but of course did not dare suggest to the Legislative committee—far more against the Democratic party than against the Republican party. In other words, the unintentional voting was confined almost entirely to our party.

Hill needed this "unintentional voting" in his quest to seize the New York party machine in 1892 and stampede the national convention. So did Tammany Hall to retain its power and pickings. While ballot reform led him closer to the machine politicians, it helped to bring the defeated Cleveland back into public prominence, strongly identified with good government and political independence. But these were incidental effects. The reform was about to sweep the nation, and the Empire State was to be included[43]

[43] D. B. Hill to Frank Jones, July 17, 1889, cit. Bass, *I am a Democrat,* 135; N. Mathews to T. S. Williams, March 14 (endorsed confidential), 1890, December 19, 1889, April 1, 1890, Timothy Shaler Williams Papers (New York Public Library, Manuscript Division). The author of the letters had drafted a bill in Massachusetts with a party column arrangement. Contrary to Hill's fears, some claimed the secret ballot would enable the Democrats to capture upstate New York and invade the traditional Republican strongholds. New York *Times,* May 10, 1888.

CHAPTER III

Throughout the Union

In drafting the first bill for the new Electoral Reform in
New York, it seemed to me that a remedy so radical
would demand years of agitation. Yet today it is the battle
cry of the Empire State. Tomorrow it bids fair to become
a practical issue of reform throughout the Union.

(Allen Thorndike Rice, 1889)

The laws must be considered, therefore, as so many adap-
tations of the Australian system.

(Joseph B. Bishop, 1892)[1]

By the end of 1889, ten American states had passed Australian
ballot laws, and fifteen legislatures had otherwise dealt with it.
It had been triumphantly vindicated in Massachusetts. It is timely
therefore to recapitulate its features:

1. The ballots were printed and distributed at public expense.

2. They contained the names of all the candidates duly nominated by law, either by party convention or petition of voters
(blanket ballot).

3. They were distributed only by the election officers at the
polling place (exclusive or official ballot).

4. There were detailed provisions for compartments and other
physical arrangements to ensure secrecy in casting the vote.

Because of these novel features, American reformers demanded
the adoption of the Australian ballot by that name as something
new. The Victorian law of 1856 and the British law of 1872 did
not simply replace oral voting with a ballot paper. Hugh Childers,
a member of the first Victorian ministry, could return to England
and say in his maiden speech to the House of Commons in 1860 in
support of the ballot, "this open or American ballot then, as giving
no protection to the voter was not established in Victoria." Victoria

[1] Allen Thorndike Rice, "The Next National Reform," *North American
Review*, CXLVIII (January, 1889), 83; Joseph B. Bishop, "The Secret
Ballot in Thirty-three States," *Forum*, XII (January, 1892), 593.

46

did establish as a precedent a detailed law providing a secret ballot and an official ballot at public expense.

It was as Wigmore observed an example of "the effective methods of modern legislation," in which an abuse was made unprofitable since the party worker could not check to see whether the bribed vote had been delivered to him. However, the number of names on the nominating petition, the arrangement of candidates on the ballot, and assistance to illiterates became contentious points of detail, and in some states were flagrantly juggled by the party machines to their own advantage.[2]

The first state law of Massachusetts was usually regarded as a model by reformers in all parts of the United States. The nominating petition required one thousand signatures for a state-wide office, and at least fifty for a district office. In order to encourage independent candidates, Wigmore felt that two signatures as in South Australia or ten as in Britain would be a feasible number for a nominating petition, as an unknown or crank candidate would not care to face ridicule. The candidates were grouped alphabetically under the title of the office with their party designated, and space was provided for write-in candidates. They were chosen by placing a cross mark in the adjoining square. An illiterate or incapacitated voter could request an election officer to assist him. The officer was bound by various penalties for breach of the act and could administer an oath to the voter.[3]

In some states the number of names required on the petition

[2] Hansard's *Parliamentary Debates,* third series, CLVI (Feb. 9, 1860), 789; Wigmore, *Australian Ballot System,* 37–38, 51–53. There is some doubt whether ten or eleven laws were enacted, as the bill in Dakota territory was reported stolen on the way to the governor! As a candidate could be unseated under the British Corrupt Practices Act of 1883, a breach of the law was especially unprofitable.

[3] *Ibid.,* 58–76; Joseph P. Harris, *Election Administration in the United States* (Washington, 1934), 174–75. "At least fifty" means that the requirement was one percent of the votes cast at the last election, but not less than fifty. Dana suggested one hundred signatures for governor, and ten to fifty for the other offices. Notes to draft bill, Dana Papers. Wigmore felt that the Australian deposit system was unfair to minor parties; but more recently Harris has criticized nominating petitions, and urged a combination of simple sponsorship and high deposit.

was made impossibly high so that the candidates would be restricted in practice to the nominees of the two major parties. The Pennsylvania law of 1891 required a candidate for state office to secure signatures equal to one-half of one percent of the last total vote cast, and for a local office equal to three percent in the district concerned. It was estimated that three thousand one hundred would be needed in Philadelphia county. The petition form was complex, and there was a fine of one thousand dollars and/or a prison sentence if a signatory was unqualified. The California law of the same year required five percent of the last total vote cast for both state and district offices. The twelve thousand five hundred signatures required to nominate a candidate for the state ticket was a drastic obstacle for the rising Prohibition and Labor parties.[4]

The Indiana law of March, 1889, introduced a new arrangement of candidates on the ballot, since known as the party column with emblem. They were grouped in parallel columns under some pictured object and it was possible to vote the whole party ticket with one mark in a circle under the emblem. Advocates of the Massachusetts law, such as Dana or Wigmore, claimed that this encouraged a sheep-like conformity and disclosed the independent voter because separate marking took longer. There were variations —the Missouri law followed the party column arrangement without a special provision for voting a straight ticket by simple method; and the Montana law, also of 1889, followed the office block arrangement, but included such provision. As the states were constantly amending their laws, the position was not clarified for two decades. By 1910, excluding the two states with no Australian ballot law, the three with compromise laws, and the two with laws of only local application, there were twenty-nine states following the party column arrangement and twelve the office block. The party was stronger than the "model" and forced such modifications in the original objectives of ballot reform. But at least the

[4] William B. Shaw, "American Ballot Reform," *Review of Reviews,* III (July, 1891), 611; Charles Chauncey Binney, "Merits and Defects of the Pennsylvania Ballot Law of 1891," *Annals of the American Academy of Political and Social Science,* II (May, 1892), 758.

laws that prescribed party column arrangement required an exclusive and official ballot. The unsatisfactory laws of Connecticut in 1889 and New York and New Jersey in 1890 retained party ballots in an effort to satisfy their governors' threats of veto. In Connecticut, the state only provided stamped paper at cost and an envelope, and the parties printed and distributed the ballots. In New York, the state itself provided separate party ballots and a blank "skin." In both cases, the peddlers could continue to operate.[5]

Apart from the objections rhetorically advanced by Governor Hill, it could be dangerous to make no provision for illiterates. In Tennessee, the lack of such provision was interpreted as an educational qualification and the law was held unconstitutional. If the provisions were loosely drawn, a bribed voter, literate or illiterate, could allow a party worker, whether a bystander or election official, to check his vote and then proceed to claim his money. The laws of New York, Pennsylvania and Maryland allowed a voter to request assistance from any qualified voter. Sometimes party workers gave the illiterate voter a printed card containing a list of candidates and the words—"I want to vote for all the candidates on this card." The effects of this abuse could be exaggerated, as many people were unwilling to admit they were illiterate and their numbers were steadily decreasing.[6]

Lawyers challenged not only the lack of aid for the illiterate, but even the principle of official ballots and detailed rules for using them. Wigmore's answer was that the constitution in thirty-three states required vote by ballot; that in legal literature and case law,

[5] Dana, "The Practical Working of the Australian Ballot in Massachusetts," 737; Ludington, *American Ballot Laws*, 84–89; Joseph B. Bishop, "Genuine and Bogus Ballot Reform," *The Nation*, LII (June 18, 1891), 491; Ivins, *On the Electoral System of the State of New York* (Albany, 1906), *passim*. Sections 14 and 22 of the Yates-Saxton bill of 1888 would have anticipated the Indiana arrangement.

[6] Joseph B. Bishop, "Successful Ballot Laws," *The Nation*, XLIX (October 17, 1889), 304; Wigmore, *Australian Ballot System*, 157; Binney, "Merits and Defects of the Pennsylvania Ballot Law of 1891," 765; Jeremiah W. Jenks, "Money in Practical Politics," *Century Illustrated Monthly Magazine*, XLIV (October, 1892), 940–52.

the word had always meant a secret vote; and that peddled and colored ballots were not secret, nor did tissue ballots provide a "free and equal vote." Accordingly, the law should strictly regulate the time and manner of voting.[7]

There was much more alarm felt about the "Tasmanian Dodge" under the highly organized American system than in the humble island of its origin. The problem was to make sure that the ballot deposited was the ballot actually received. If the official initialed the back, that would prevent stuffing; but a capable team of "dodgers" could vote for pay and lose only their first ballot. To place the voter's name or roll-number on a numbered counterfoil and then check back with the ballot number before deposit would be effective, but could impair secrecy. So various provisions were contrived for removing and destroying the stub containing the ballot number.

If the party machines were prepared to support or to mangle the laws, they did so impartially. The compromise laws were forced by the vetoes of Governor Morgan S. Bulkeley, Republican of Connecticut, and Governor David B. Hill, Democrat of New York. If the Democrats gained most from malpractice in New York, the Republicans gained most from it in Indiana in 1888, and the Democrats took the lead in pushing the reform in the next session. Wigmore tabulated the legislative votes for 1888–89. He found that the vote followed party lines in six states and ran across them in eighteen. If each party received one point for providing a majority for the bill, or for being the minority when it was defeated, the score was Democrats, fourteen and Republicans, ten.[8]

The actual initiative in promoting the reform generally followed the pattern in Massachusetts. Here, the chief petitioners were the Mugwumps, or bolters of 1884 and advocates of civil service reform. They were aided by labor groups, influenced by Henry

[7] Wigmore, *Australian Ballot System*, 185–99; Wigmore, "Ballot Reform: its Constitutionality," *American Law Review*, XXIII (September–October, 1889), 719–32. The nature of the mark used also produced many court cases.

[8] Wigmore, *Australian Ballot System*, 23–49, 205; *Public Opinion*, January 11, 1890.

George, who in some states took the primary initiative. Their chief opponents were the leaders of the Boston Irish who ran the Democratic party machine and feared the loosening of old ethnic and party ties.[9]

Whatever the progress made and whichever parties, major or minor, were responsible, it was inconceivable that a great reform could bypass New York. The legislative session of 1890 and the electoral system of the state attracted nation-wide attention. In his annual message, Governor Hill again devoted a great part of it to electoral reform, but again adamantly opposed an exclusive or official ballot and any hindrance to illiterates. The New York *Sun,* champion of Hill and the party machine, contrasted "this new scheme of disfranchisement" of the Mugwump element with "universal manhood suffrage, the pride and glory of the Empire State."[10]

The legislature promptly received and passed the Saxton bill again, and a giant petition was being circulated among the people. The trend was unmistakable. The Governor sought to hedge, first, by suggesting that they seek an informal opinion from the court, and then on March 31 by issuing his third veto. For a month the governor and the leaders of the Republican majority jockeyed for advantage. Eventually Hill and the Ballot Reform League devised a compromise bill which passed both houses unanimously. The ballots were to be distributed by the election officials and paid for by the state. The voter received at the polling place separate party ballots and a blank containing the titles of the offices. He could elect to use one of the official ballots, or affix a paster ballot obtained privately to the blank. The ballots were then folded alike and the unused placed for discard. The pasters satisfied the governor's objections, but their use by illiterates and others simply

[9] *Supra,* 36–40; Geoffrey T. Blodgett, *The Gentle Reformers: Massachusetts Democrats in the Cleveland Era* (Cambridge, 1966), 116.

[10] New York *Sun,* cit. *Public Opinion,* January 11, 1890; *Public Papers of David B. Hill,* 1890, 7–34. He made some comments on the Anglo-Australian system, apparently unaware that four of the six Australian colonies at this time had manhood suffrage for the lower house. *Ibid.,* 9–10.

invited the parties to retain the practices of peddling and assessments to cover the cost. Saxton criticized the law and urged New York to adopt the Massachusetts law with an office block, blanket ballot. By contrast, Hill claimed a victory over the "doctrinaires" and "barnacles" of electoral reform: "The new method may be more appropriately styled the American reform election system, because it aims at practical rather than theoretical reform, and is in consonnance with our American theory of government."[11]

The two men clashed in the elections of 1894 when Hill returned from the United States Senate to run unsuccessfully for another term as governor and Saxton ran successfully for lieutenant-governor on the Republican ticket. The lengthy report of a committee chaired by State Senator Clarence Lexow charged the New York City police with conniving at repeating, intimidation and other abuses on a huge scale. The reformers were given the ammunition to press for the replacement of the compromise law with an effective Australian ballot law. With little fuss, Governor Levi P. Morton in May, 1895, signed a bill which introduced a blanket ballot with party column and emblem.[12]

The Australian ballot received a stiff test in the presidential elections of the following year. Although Hill was prepared to abide by the result of the party convention, there were many Gold Democrats in the state who refused to do so. In addition, the New York *Times,* Bowker, and most of the Mugwump and independent elements, forgetting their acrimonious disputes over the tariff, were now firmly behind McKinley and the Republican ticket. The ballot was certainly complex. There were eight columns—the Republican ticket under an eagle; the Democratic under a star;

11 New York *Times,* May 1–3, 1890; Charles Saxton, "Changes in the Ballot Law," *North American Review,* CLII (June, 1891), 753–56; *Public Papers of David B. Hill,* 1890, 33.

12 *The Nation,* LVIII (January 4, 1894), 4; W. T. Stead, *Satan's Invisible World Displayed: or Despairing Democracy* (New York, 1897), 192–202. It is no coincidence that in the year of publication, the Citizens Union was formed to support Seth Low as first mayor of Greater New York. The noted English journalist stirred up support for the Mugwump reformers and their continuing efforts as he had done in another city with *If Christ Came to Chicago* in 1894.

the National Democratic under a ship; the Prohibition under a fountain; the Socialist Labor under an arm and hammer; the People's party under a three-leaf clover; the Independents under a bullock; and there was a column for write ins. The sample in the press gave two hundred fifty-two names for thirty-six presidential electors and six important offices in each of six columns. In addition, there were various local offices. There was some confusion about what would happen if a voter put a cross under the party emblem and then chose a few individual candidates. A Supreme Court judge said that voting a split ticket was beyond his understanding. So several party leaders opened schools to instruct voters in this new and difficult art.[13]

As the election loomed, the "sound money" parade of October 31 was described through several pages of print; while Bryan was persistently dismissed as a "demagogue" and "cunning knave," oozing fire and wind by turns. But although this was a particularly complex and heated election, it was, at least in New York, generally well conducted. The turnout in the city was high and gave the Republicans their first presidential win there. The police were attentive and enforced the law prohibiting electioneering within one hundred feet of a polling place; but there were few heelers and rowdies to trouble them. Casting his mind back, the press reporter seemed puzzled—"facially it was not possible to determine who was an advocate of McKinley or Bryan."[14]

"This is strictly the people's cause," wrote William B. Shaw in July, 1891. "It commands no paid lobby, no 'barrels,' no 'influence.' It succeeds without these agencies only because the people in many States are known to stand behind it." It is now possible to ask how the movement for the Australian ballot spread, and how did "the people in many States" come to stand behind a measure which in 1888 was seriously canvased only in Massachusetts and New York?[15]

Most students of politics these days are sceptical of spontaneous

13 New York *Times,* November 1–2, 1896.
14 *Ibid.,* November 1, 4, 1896.
15 Shaw, "American Ballot Reform," 609.

53

eruptions of "the people." They look for elites, leaders and followers, and pressure groups. Two distinct groups, the Mugwumps
and Single Taxers, usually took the lead in pressing for the Australian ballot and were already organized for reform in many
states. The politics of New York and her periodical press com-
manded nation-wide attention. This enhanced the political influence of the Mugwumps. A national political figure might
identify himself with the cause. As the Populist party in any
textbook appears to dominate the 1890's, and as they were capable
of arousing much zeal, it is also worth asking how far they guided
this particular reform.

The Australian ballot was one of several reforms which appeared in the Populist platform and was later generally accepted.
Some historians praise the agrarian crusaders for their foresight
and energy while others find that they borrowed their ideas extensively from the eastern cities. The argument can be overworked
for such a reform changed from a fad to a movement very quickly.
New ideas were rapidly disseminated by a growing periodical press.
The pioneers had drawn from different sources—Walthew of
Michigan had looked to Canada; Ivins of New York to Britain;
and Wallace of Louisville to Australia, as described by Henry
George. In the sessions of 1889 in several states, a number of bills
were introduced before the legislatures by different people acting
independently. The decision of an isolated armchair reformer, repeated many times, gave the impression of a gust of public opinion,
just as the decision of many isolated farmers as they perused the
new mail-order catalogs indicated popular taste.[16]

[16] John D. Hicks, *The Populist Revolt* (Minneapolis, 1931), 403–07, and
passim; Chester McA. Destler, "Western Radicalism, 1865–1901: Concepts
and Origins," *Mississippi Valley Historical Review,* XXXI (December,
1944), 133–68. Destler includes the Locofoco, Greenback and Populist
movements as part of a continuing opposition to monopoly; but he gives
only one example of urban initiative at this time, the adoption of the
initiative-referendum in the Omaha platform. Wigmore in 1889 drew attention to the different sources and motives, and the need for organized
opinion. "A Summary of Ballot Reform," *The Nation,* XLIX (August 29,
1889), 165–66. For Dana's "discovery," see "Sir William Vernon Harcourt and the Australian Ballot Law," 410.

The older eastern centers of wealth and publication were well placed to influence public opinion. A major speech or a major bill might receive editorial comment around the nation; for example, *Public Opinion* clipped seventeen varied papers to praise the first trial of the Massachusetts law. An alert local editor might emulate the Providence *Journal,* which commented not only on Massachusetts, but also on the bills in Montana and Connecticut. Another means of communication and guidance was the periodicals, published mainly in New York, and attracting a wider and more responsive audience. This study frequently mentions the *North American Review,* the *Century Illustrated Monthly Magazine, Harper's Weekly, Forum* and the *Nation,* and editors such as E. L. Godkin of the New York *Evening Post* (1881–99), and Allen Thorndike Rice of the *North American Review.* Founder-editor of the *Nation* and still influencing the policy of the sister-weekly, Godkin had a potent style and a breathless following among the Mugwump element. Above all, he had a remarkable influence over other editors. Richard Watson Gilder of the *Century* (1881–1909) was more self-effacing; but he frequently mentioned ballot reform in his editorial topics, and with the "Battles and Leaders" series, Nicolay and Hay's "Lincoln," and fine illustration and production, had built up a large circulation of two hundred thousand to read them.[17]

The timing of press support is important in creating support for an issue. Ivins' addresses were followed by articles in three con-

[17] *Public Opinion,* November 16, 1889; Mott, *American Magazines,* II, *passim;* The *Century* circulation was exceptional, but inside five years it was being left behind by *McLure's* and others. *Harper's* circulation was one hundred thousand and slipping; the weekly *Nation* only ten thousand; Rice moved the *North American Review* from Boston to New York and built up the circulation from one thousand two hundred to seventeen thousand. On Godkin's influence, see Rollo Ogden, *Life and Letters of Edwin Lawrence Godkin,* 2 vols. (New York, 1907), II, 230; Oswald Garrison Villard, *Fighting Years: Memoirs of a Liberal Editor* (New York, 1939), 123; Henry Holt, *Garrulities of an Octagenarian Editor* (New York, 1923), 287–88. In his concluding chapter, Daniel Aaron refers to the "receptive readership" of the late-nineteenth century. *Men of Good Hope: the Story of the American Progressives* (New York, 1951), 305.

secutive numbers of the *Nation*. In commenting on the trial in Massachusetts, the *Century* waited until January, 1890, to warn readers about the coming struggle in New York and the further reforms which the ballot portended.

Active individuals and their personal publications were also important in stirring up opinion. Wigmore, in the Preface to the second edition of his book, asked people to send him a copy of any ballot reform bill and a history of the agitation in their state. However, no further edition appeared after 1889 as he had accepted a chair of law at Tokyo University. The Society for Political Education, founded in 1880 by Richard Rogers Bowker of New York, published *Electoral Reform* in 1889 as one of its regular Economic Tracts. It was probably written by Bowker himself, a publisher and then chairman of the Society. From scattered portions of his papers, the distribution of the Tracts can be estimated. A circular in 1883 claimed that the membership was one thousand four hundred scattered over every state and territory, and for his fee of fifty cents each member received the four yearly tracts. The Society occasionally sent its publications to two hundred eighty colleges and high schools and four hundred newspapers, and received the active cooperation of the publishers, Henry Holt and George Haven Putnam. Bowker also published *The Peoples Cause: a Journal of Tariff Reform, Ballot Reform and Civil Service Reform,* which appeared in twelve monthly issues during 1889. Such a publication encouraged the reader to regard these reforms as a national movement. It contained not only articles but lists of books and articles and information about legislation and reform clubs elsewhere.[18]

But the way to really attract attention was for a national figure to commit himself, as Grover Cleveland had emphasized tariff reform in his annual message of December, 1887. Two years later, the now defeated candidate was asked to give an address to the

[18] R. L. Dugdale to Bowker, October 24, 1881, Iles to Bowker, November 24, 1890, S. P. E. Letterbook, Bowker Papers. By 1890, Bowker was told that there were only one hundred twenty-two subscribers and they were facing competition from the improved periodicals.

Merchants Association of Boston. Cleveland decided to take a strong stand on ballot reform and sent for George F. Parker who had done some editorial work for the Democratic party in the last campaign. As Cleveland refused to hedge in any way, Parker suggested he go the whole hog and place five hundred copies ahead of time with the press associations.

The speech was composed with his usual dogged sincerity and delivered on December 12, 1889. The theme was political selfishness. Ballot reform would check the bribery and intimidation which stems from self-interest, he said, but could not destroy the root. Much praise was due Massachusetts for her leadership in ballot as in civil service reform. Cleveland was of course implying that the protected manufacturers were almost identical with the selfish, and like Godkin and Bowker he persistently linked ballot and tariff reform. The effect of the speech was electric and coincided with the widely publicized opposition of another leading Democrat, Senator Arthur P. Gorman of Maryland. *Public Opinion* clipped forty-two newspapers around the nation which supported the reform. Cleveland himself received a growing number of speaking engagements and Parker became a sort of press secretary. As the Australian ballot became the law in state after state, Cleveland's speech was revealed as the unintentional opening shot of his triumphant nomination over Hill and return to office in 1892.[19]

So the movement spread. The farm and labor organizations supported most reforms intended to make legislatures more responsive to the will of the mass of the people and the nostrums presented in their name. The twelfth item of the platform adopted by the Northern Farmers Alliance at St. Louis in December, 1889, read: "We favour the Australian system, or some similar system of voting, and ask for enactment of laws regulating the nomination of candidates for public office."

The proposals in earlier platforms were endorsed by the inde-

[19] George F. Parker ed., *Writings and Speeches of Grover Cleveland* (New York, 1892), 148–55, 344; George F. Parker, *Recollections of Grover Cleveland* (New York, 1911), 125–28; *Public Opinion,* January 11, 1890. The *Peoples Cause* frequently connected tariff and ballot reform; see for example, June 1889, 78.

pendent and national third party formed by the Alliances, Union Labor party and Knights of Labor at Cincinnati in May, 1891, and generally known as the Populist party. When they met in Omaha the following year to select a presidential candidate, the Australian ballot was included among a number of resolutions attached to the platform drafted by Ignatius Donnelly, lecturer for the Alliance in Minnesota. It was suggested by the grievances so fiercely indicated in the preamble: "We meet in the midst of a nation brought to the verge of moral, political and material ruin. Corruption dominates the ballot box, the legislatures, the Congress, and touches even the ermine of the bench. . . ."

However, the concern displayed by the Alliances and Populists was weak and variable. Professor John D. Hicks in his standard work lists eight southern and two prairie states in which Alliance candidates won control after the elections of 1890. The ballot law was carried in the session of 1891 only in Nebraska, where the local Alliance had an active educational program. The party prepared bills in Kansas, but did not control the upper house. This was remedied at the next election, but now the control of the lower house depended on several contested seats. For a hectic month, the partisans took turns barricading themselves inside the hall while the new Democrat-Populist governor called up the militia and the Republicans swore in deputies. Finally the courts intervened, as the legislators seemed incapable. The victorious Republican party adopted the Australian ballot and other reforms in order to confront the fusion of Democrats and Populists and it readily passed in the session of 1893. The Alliance had won the battle but lost the campaign. So much for Kansas and Nebraska. This group of ten Alliance-controlled states also included South Carolina and Georgia, which were the two remaining states yet to adopt the reform in 1910.[20]

[20] Hicks, *Populist Revolt*, 178–85, 210, 405–07, Appendix A; *Appleton's Annual Encyclopaedia and Register of Important Events for 1890*, 299–301; St. Louis *Post-Dispatch*, December 2–8, 1889, which paper approved several planks including the Australian ballot; W. F. Rightmire, "The Alliance Movement in Kansas: Origins of the People's Party," *Kansas State Historical Society Collections*, IX (1906), 1–8; William F. Zornow,

For the elections of 1892, the ardent southern radical, Tom Watson of Georgia, produced *The People's Party Campaign Book.* This is described as "a brief statement of the line of argument which we adopt upon all essential issues." In four hundred pages of comment, roll calls, speeches and editorials, there is no mention of the Australian ballot. The *National Economist,* official organ first of the (southern) National Alliance and then of the National Farmers Alliance and Industrial Union, a well-produced weekly published in Washington, has only one article discussing the reform. It is a summary of an article by Edward Wakefield of New Zealand which appeared in the *Forum.*[21]

In some states, the agrarian element proved a useful ally. In Dakota territory, the Alliance presented one bill and strongly supported another, which was passed but strangely disappeared on its way to the governor. The parties were so evenly balanced in the Illinois legislature in 1891 that three members acknowledging the support of the Farmers Mutual Benefit Association held the balance of power, while a number of the partisan members had also received their endorsement. Pressure also came from the Mugwump element. On January 2, 1891, the Chicago Ballot Reform League was established, with Jesse Cox, a prominent lawyer, as secretary. Cox explained a draft bill based on the Minnesota law which would be presented at the forthcoming session. Both parties indicated their support. On March 21, Reed Green, a young Democrat and lawyer from Cairo, reported out seven bills and a substitute bill for the house committee on elections, and the latter was brought to the floor. The April elections in Chicago were held under the old law and the presence of five candidates for mayor encouraged more than the usual intimidation and fraud.

Kansas: a History of the Jayhawk State (Norman, 1957), 198–203; J. M. Thompson, "The Farmers Alliance in Nebraska: Something of its Origins, Growth and Influence," *Proceedings and Collections of the Nebraska State Historical Society,* X (1902), 202–03.

21 Thomas E. Watson, *The People's Party Campaign Book, 1892* (Washington, 1892). There is an incomplete run of the nine volumes of the *National Economist* (1889–93) in the Library of Congress. Wakefield's article is discussed in the issue of October 12, 1889.

The Australian Ballot:

The "shoulder-strikers" of the first ward systematically swept the independent Democrats from their domain. The *Daily Tribune* decided to investigate one precinct thoroughly and found a turnout of 545 out of 564 voters, of whom 502 had voted the regular Democratic ticket. Several names were repeated on the roll, and the post office returned one hundred forty-seven letters after a mailing to all the voters. So the press and victorious Republicans in the city joined the agitation. The ballot law was passed unanimously by the house; but the Republican majority in the Senate wanted the opportunity to investigate and remove fraudulent ballots in Chicago. Eventually a conference committee reached a compromise—the ballots were not numbered but to be retained for six months. The amendments were passed unanimously on June 10, and the following day the legislature passed a bill to amend the registration provisions of the city election law.[22]

The Minnesota law used by Cox had been passed in the session of 1889 by a legislature with a large Republican majority. The Alliance members held the balance of power in 1891 and were able to extend it over the state and secure an election-day holiday. The author of both bills was John A. Keyes, Republican. In 1894 and 1896, he ran unsuccessfully for attorney-general on the Populist ticket. In later years, he advocated the initiative and referendum and public ownership of monopolies, and joined the Socialist party.[23]

As the Alliance claimed a membership of three million, with more than one hundred thousand in each of several states, they were obviously a potent force if led and informed. The National Farmers Alliance and Industrial Union, the title adopted by the Southern Alliance in December, 1889, when it absorbed the Agricultural Wheel and other bodies, maintained salaried officers in Washington and published a well-produced weekly, the *National Economist,* edited by C. W. Macune.

[22] Chicago *Daily Tribune,* January 3–4, March 23, April 8–11, June 11, 1891.
[23] Frank R. Holmes, *Minnesota in Three Centuries,* 4 vols. (New York, 1908), IV, 155–82, 205.

It is easy to be misled by the emotional and class-conscious tone of some Populist writings and speeches. The same can be found in the official organ of the Alliance. But the effects were muted by the wide definition of "producers"; by the emphasis on education in agricultural techniques and public affairs; and by insisting that members could act either through the Populist party or the major parties. After the presidential elections of November, 1892, Macune simply said: "The people do not want any radical law or violent changes. They are opposed to class legislation of any kind. If the Democratic party will return to the original principles of democracy it can perpetuate itself for a quarter of a century." In practice, the Populists helped to promote if they did not initiate the Australian ballot and other specific reforms.[24]

The emotion was certainly there. Mary Lease told the farmers of Kansas to "raise less corn and more hell!" Ignatius Donnelly, former Congressman and now a professional lecturer for the Alliance, published a novel in 1890 entitled *Caesar's Column: a Story of the Twentieth Century*. It luridly described the revolution that would follow thwarted reform, and used quotations from actual articles published in the 1880's. With New York virtually destroyed in the fighting, the ogre-like Caesar ordered his gang to pile up the bodies and coat them with concrete as a pleasant memento of the victory. However the narrator, accompanied by a few noble companions and a lady love, had already departed for a destination in Africa. In this Populist utopia, the purity of elections was highly regarded. Donnelly repeated a warning issued by the *Century* in 1889 about the consequences of bribery and fraudulent voting. The new order treated such things as high treason and a capital offense, although minor offenders might simply be disfranchised.

As the novel was written under the pseudonym of Boisgilbert, many authors and reformers were saddled with the authorship. It was attributed to Judge Albion W. Tourgée, Andrew Carnegie, Jared Ingersoll, Bishop Henry C. Potter, Judge Lyman Trumbull, Edward Bellamy, Mark Twain, Edward Everett Hale, William

[24] *National Economist,* November 19, 1892.

The Australian Ballot:

Dean Howells and others, including Donnelly. The "sage of Nininger" was in fine company.[25]

The other minor parties were associated with the work of Henry George and labor leaders such as Robert Schilling. In 1889, Wigmore was able to give a concise summary of legislative activity in twenty-five states. In most of them a local labor organization, a Single Tax branch or George's paper, the *Standard,* had been prominent. For example, in Missouri, the Single Tax League drafted the House bill which James B. ("Champ") Clark introduced and for which he afterwards claimed the credit. The Senate bill was drafted by the Civil Service Reform Association. George and Schilling were not Socialists; they remained within that tradition of reform which emphasized individual opportunity and self-respect. Although monopoly and a negative laissez-faire attitude might arouse their anger, they made many specific proposals in common with the Mugwump or Good Government elements of New York and Boston.[26]

Labor leaders and reformers were particularly disturbed by the prospect that the burgeoning factories and cities would make it easier for employers to coerce the votes of their workingmen.

[25] Ignatius Donnelly, *Caesar's Column: a Story of the Twentieth Century,* ed. Walter B. Rideout (Cambridge, 1960), 302 and *passim;* F. J. Shulte to I. Donnelly, March 4, 1890, Donnelly Papers (Minnesota Historical Society, St. Paul). Donnelly at this time was still giving his well-paid lectures on the Baconian theory of Shakespeare. It seems to be stretching a point to claim as Victor S. Ferkiss does that the Populists supported the Australian ballot, direct election of Senators, and similar reforms in common with other groups in order to secure direct, plebiscitary democracy, and were thus harbingers of Fascism. Some agrarian radicals like William Lemke may later have become soured and over borne by their isolationism, emotions and disdain for parliamentary methods. "The Political and Economic Philosophy of American Fascism" (Unpublished doctoral dissertation, University of Chicago, 1954), 335–36.

[26] Wigmore, *Australian Ballot System,* 23–47. Clark is best known as the Speaker of the House of Representatives between 1911 and 1919 and the leading challenger to Woodrow Wilson for the Democratic presidential nomination in 1912. In his book, *My Quarter Century of American Politics,* 2 vols. (New York, 1920), I, 115, II, 20, he categorically states he was the author of the Missouri Australian ballot law. The above is taken from Wigmore's contemporary account.

Terence Powderly recorded his experience of politics in Scranton, Pennsylvania:

> Fancy a man who had a family depending on him for support daring to accept a ticket from the man who peddled tickets for a party that the boss of mine or workshop did not favor. . . . It was that condition of affairs, more than anything else, that brought me into politics in 1876 and from that day until it became an accomplished fact I fought for the adoption of a secret ballot.

In that year, the twenty-seven-year-old machinist joined the Knights of Labor and also the Greenback party. By printing tickets at cost and organizing a team to distribute them and watch the polls, the new party was able to take several county offices. In February, 1878, Powderly was elected mayor of Scranton and served three terms. However, it is as Grand Master Workman of the Knights from 1879 to 1893 that he is better known, rather than as one of many forgotten agitators for the Australian ballot reform in various parts of the union.[27]

[27] Terence V. Powderly, *The Path I Trod,* ed. Harry J. Carman *et al.* (New York, 1940), 67–73, 174.

CHAPTER IV

Preparatory to the Revision of the Suffrage

The election bill is necessary to insure fair and honest elections under the present suffrage qualifications, and it should become a law as a measure preparatory to the revision of the suffrage provisions in the constitution.

> (New Orleans *Daily Picayune,*
> 1896)

Three cheers for the Good Government League!

> (Henry Clay Warmoth, governor
> of Louisiana during
> Reconstruction)

. . . California—a State on which I dwell the more willingly because it is in many respects the most striking in the whole Union. . . .

> (James Bryce, 1888)[1]

The preceding chapters have discussed the origins of the Australian ballot reform, the reasons for its adoption, the individuals or groups who promoted it, and its dissemination. The most important contribution was made by the Mugwumps and Single Taxers, and the first, decisive battles were fought in New York and Massachusetts, both northeastern states. The passage of the reform there has been described in some detail. To provide a balance, two states in two other regions, California, in the Far West, and Louisiana in the South will be discussed. Once again, the passage of the reform sheds light on the characteristics of the states concerned and fills out the extraordinary variety of American political forms and style. The distinctiveness of southern politics including election laws and practice almost constitutes a system in itself, which justifies separate treatment.

[1] New Orleans *Daily Picayune,* June 23, April 8, 1896; Bryce, *American Commonwealth,* II, 426. Warmoth was only thirty when his term expired in 1872, and appeared on and off in local politics for the next forty years. He wrote his memoirs as recently as 1930 insisting that he was not a Carpetbagger but a Scallawag of southern family.

Preparatory to the Revision of the Suffrage

In a famous passage, James Bryce described the West as the land of glowing promise and the most American part of America. "California" meant a golden utopia in the Spanish legends, and, as the farthest West, has for over one hundred years revealed the nation to itself in brighter colors. The passage of her Australian ballot law and the aftermath is full of interest. Party politics in California in the 1850's were conducted with the usual methods and abuses, but with a pristine vigor all their own. The epic struggle between Tammany and Chivalry has already been used for illustration. After the sudden riches of the gold rush, the state fell on hard times. The explosion came at the meetings held on the sandlots opposite the city hall in San Francisco, where a fiery Irishman named Dennis Kearney directed the wrath of the crowds against the Chinese and the greedy corporations which employed them. The Workingmen's party was able to gain one-third of the seats at the constitutional convention of 1878, and forced the fusion of the major parties in opposition. The practical results were slight and the real locus of power became even more firmly fixed in the hands of the Southern Pacific railroad company and those who controlled it. By 1890, the railroad had a stranglehold over all transportation, had accumulated a generous endowment of land and mineral resources, and bent an indulgent and greedy legislature and judiciary to its will.[2]

The first specific proposal for the Australian ballot in the United States was made by Henry George in 1871 while embroiled in California party politics. (California also inspired his *Progress and Poverty*.) In 1889, the measure was promoted by a mixed group of reformers and defeated by the party machines in combination. The bill slipped through in the session of 1891, when the trained seals of the legislature were performing with unusual brilliance. Their extravagances expressed, if in a somewhat distorted way, the restless and speculative temper of the people of a state which had grown up "like a gourd in the night." Reform and acquisitiveness will coexist among such a people. The novels of protest of Frank Norris, Helen Hunt Jackson, Jack London

[2] Bryce, *American Commonwealth*, II, 426–48, 681; George Mowry, *The California Progressives* (Berkeley, 1951), 1–22.

and John Steinbeck will vie with the soothing invocations to "the loved one."[3]

Four bills were presented independently in the session of 1889. Two came from members of the Assembly; one from the San Francisco Federation of Trades and Labor Organisations, with the aid of the New York *Standard;* and another from the Young Mens Democratic League. The latter passed a third reading in the Assembly, but was strangely defeated on a motion to re-consider. The parties split evenly on both votes.[4]

The Republicans swept the next elections and entered the session of 1891 with a three-to-one majority in both houses. However, Governor Henry H. Markham in his message of January 7 did not seem anxious to commit himself on the Australian ballot, or anything else. He said that he had no opinion for or against it; but if they considered it necessary to improve the election laws, they should retain the good features of the present, and incorporate the good features of some other system! On the same day, three bills were introduced by assemblymen from San Francisco including one based on the Massachusetts law and promoted again by the Federated Trades. A number of bills were introduced in the Senate. Several bills were combined and the final bill passed both houses on March 20.[5]

However, the legislature spent most of its time electing two United States Senators, including Leland Stanford, former governor of California and a former president of the Southern Pacific, and investigating a charge that an assemblyman had accepted a bribe from a would-be policeman anxious for a reference. Another investigation was necessary when a bundle of greenback wrappers found in the wastebasket of the state library was

[3] Bryce, *American Commonwealth,* II, 372.

[4] Wigmore, *Australian Ballot System,* 42–43. The press did not seem much concerned.

[5] San Francisco *Daily Evening Bulletin,* January 8, March 25–26, 1891. The paper was Republican-Mugwump, and played the role of the New York *Evening Post* on the west coast. A number of bills went into the legislative hopper, and it is difficult to ascertain the author of the final measure.

traced back to the railroad's bank account. At the tail end of the session, the legislature decided to hand the documents to the governor, thus killing the issue, and whitewashed the greedy assemblyman by accepting a minority report which simply found him negligent.

In addition, there were at least two brawls during the session. In a midnight encounter at a hotel, the "sage of Tehama" passed a slur on the Irish whereupon the "Vallejo statesman" swung a punch. His sixty-five-year-old rival, clearly the more sober, felled him with one blow. Summing up, the *Daily Evening Bulletin* of San Francisco described the legislature as sound only on Stanfordism, and "more prolific of scandals than any legislature that ever sat in California." This was a high standard to match. As the paper added, why they held firm on the Australian ballot law was a mystery.[6]

One of the real pioneers of California, John Bidwell, was a member of the first organized immigration party to reach the state in 1841. He became a prosperous farmer and an active politician over a period of forty years. It is not certain whether Bidwell as a state senator helped to justify the colloquial description of the first legislature as "the legislature of a thousand drinks," but he embraced the Prohibition party later in life and was their candidate for president in 1892. In the previous year, the bearded, seventy-two-year-old pioneer had been interviewed by the indefatigable publisher-historian, Hubert Howe Bancroft. He said:

> The Australian ballot system to me is the most important; I believe that no political party at this time appreciates its value . . . I almost believe that system is so important that the existence of our country depends upon it. I believe that if the people can express themselves, if they can exercise their intelligence, let it be intelligence small or great, if they can only exercise that intelligence—the intelligence itself will grow. What does any ballot mean here? Here's a democratic ballot. Not one man in 20 cares a fig for all the names. Every one perhaps has a favourite. A few intelligent men may want to

[6] San Francisco *Daily Evening Bulletin,* March 25–26, 1891; San Francisco *Alta California,* January 15, 1891.

vote their own ticket and see every one elected, but if a man does not care anything about those names and puts in the ticket simply because it is the party ticket, how much of an expression of his will is that? Under the Aus. ballot, a man is obliged to exercise his intelligence. He reads the first name. He knows whether it is republican or otherwise, because the party name is printed right opposite. . . . He goes into a room by himself, and he exercises his own good judgment in regard to the man he wants to vote for.

The New York liberals and reformers could hardly have put the case better.[7]

Ballot reform produced the same improvements in California as elsewhere. But her most distinctive and unusual contribution was to come. In the early twentieth century, the Progressives organized the Lincoln-Roosevelt League which swept the Republican primaries in 1911, and then the final elections. They made a fetish of independency and saddled the state from 1913 to 1959 with her extraordinary cross-filing law. The results of this procedure also indicate how the form of the ballot can influence the voters' behavior.[8]

The California Progressives were evidently dubious about the future of the new party and aimed to capture the votes of the reformers and regulars together. The direct primary law of 1909 was amended in 1913 to allow a candidate for partisan office to seek the nomination of parties with which he was not personally affiliated by registration. The law was changed in 1917 to require the candidate to win the nomination of his own party. This led to unfortunate consequences in the following year when James Rolph secured the Democratic but failed to win his own Republican party nomination. The Democrats were left without a

[7] Bidwell Dictation, 1891, 37–39, Bancroft Papers (Bancroft Library, University of California, Berkeley).

[8] Evelyn Hazen, *Cross Filing in Primary Elections,* Bureau of Public Administration Legislative Problems No. 4 (Berkeley, 1951); Robert J. Pichell, "The Electoral System and Voting Behaviour: the Case of California's Cross-Filing," *Western Political Science Quarterly,* XII (June, 1959), 459–84; tables provided by the office of Mr. Frank Jordan, Secretary of State for California. When Dr. Hazen wrote in 1951, the system was permitted but little used in Maine and Vermont.

candidate for governor, so the law was further changed to permit a party's central committee to fill the vacancy. There was no party designation on the primary ballot; and in 1935, it was provided that the name of incumbents would be listed first. The system was now complete.

With the decline of the third or Progressive party in the state, many candidates of the major parties made cross-filing their major objective. Between 1918 and 1950, one-half of the candidates elected to the Assembly and over three-fifths elected to the state Senate cross-filed successfully. That is, they were then and there elected at the primary as in the southern one-party states, but for different reasons. As the voter was reading mere names, the system favored incumbents, prominent people, and the selection of the press. In 1950, the last elections before a major change in the law, one hundred eighty-six of the two hundred twenty-four candidates for the eighty Assembly seats cross-filed, fifty-eight successfully. Of the fifty-eight, thirty-one were Republicans and twenty-seven Democrats, and fifty-three of the fifty-eight were incumbents. The percentage of the successful cross-filers was here about seventy-two, compared with fifty as the average over the period from 1918 to 1950. Significantly, the number of successful cross-filers was at its lowest in 1932, a year of acute social tension.[9]

The tradition of Hiram Johnson and bipartisan reform also hung over the executive. In 1946, Earl Warren, now the Chief Justice of the United States, won both party nominations for governor, and Goodwin Knight repeated the feat four years later as lieutenant-governor. The controller and secretary of state cross-filed successfully in seven of the ten primaries up to 1950. By this time, the Democratic party had emerged from a long period of decline, and their number of registered voters exceeded the opposition. However, most candidates concentrated on gathering an impressive combined total at the primaries hoping to break their opponents' confidence.

The turnout at these primary elections was sometimes alarmingly low, and averaged only fifty-three percent over the period

[9] Hazen, *Cross Filing,* 18, 20.

from 1918 to 1950, compared with an average of seventy-three percent at the general elections. Where so many candidates cross-filed successfully and were elected by such a scanty turnout using almost identical ballots, the elections provided only a very limited expression of opinion. There was less and less significance in the party label and the act of registration. Bills to abolish the practice had been introduced since 1919, but they had been blocked in committee or the unrepresentative Senate amid dire warnings of a return to boss rule. The call for "party responsibility" was equally insistent. In 1951, an initiative measure was sent to the legislature, which instead put a compromise proposal on the ballot requiring a party designation after the candidates' names. This was accepted by the voters and came into operation for the elections of 1954. A most remarkable change now took place. In the elections of 1952, fourteen United States representatives, eighteen of the twenty state senators, and sixty-two of the eighty state assemblymen had cross-filed successfully; now, only two representatives, eleven senators and twenty-two assemblymen did so when wearing their party clothes. Edmund "Pat" Brown, Democrat, and William Knowland, Republican, cross-filed for the gubernatorial nominations in June, 1958. Brown received about twenty-three percent and Knowland about fourteen percent of the total votes cast in the respective opposition primary. By the time that Governor Brown and Richard Nixon waged their vigorous match four years later, cross-filing had been abolished. About 108,000 write-in votes—less than three percent of the total—were cast in the opposition primaries for Brown, Nixon and Joseph Shell. The turnout was sixty-four percent, compared with the average of fifty-three percent under the old procedure. The party label and contests of national significance have pulled most voters firmly into their party, and in times of difficulty they need not turn to the extravagances of "Epic" and "Ham and Eggs."[10]

10 See fn. 8; Secretary of State, California, *Statement of Vote: Direct Primary Election* (Sacramento, 1958, 1962). "Epic" stood for End Poverty in California, the slogan of the novelist Upton Sinclair in his campaign for governor in 1934, and "Ham and Eggs" described a fanciful pension scheme about the same time.

The other features of the modern California ballot are worth noting. They have an office block arrangement with detachable stub and the voters choose their candidates by a cross mark made with the rubber stamp provided. Judicial, school and fiscal offices are placed together in a separate nonpartisan section of the ballot, without party labels. The state ticket of six headed by the governor, the Board of Equalization, and the national and state legislators remain as partisan offices. In presidential years, there is a convention primary and a short ballot for the national candidates. The form of the ballot, while encouraging a greater awareness of party, still encourages independency.

A quite different atmosphere surrounds ballot reform in the South, and Louisiana has been chosen for precise illustration. A heavy Reconstruction debt, a dependence upon staple products, and a high proportion of rural population were characteristic of the whole South. But Louisiana at the turn of the century also had the highest illiteracy rate in the nation, for half of her people were colored and some of the Cajuns or rural French took a fierce pride in retaining their native tongue. The proportion of people classified as rural was unusually high at seventy-three percent, yet most of the city dwellers lived in New Orleans, whose population of two hundred eighty-seven thousand far exceeded that of the second largest city, Shreveport, with sixteen thousand. The proportion of tenant occupiers was unusually high, many of whom were virtually plantation laborers tilling contiguous lots and hopelessly in debt. The southern part of the state was greatly influenced by the French-Catholic tradition and politically dominated by the merchants of New Orleans and the sugar planters. The governing class also included the planters of the Red and Mississippi River valleys, who could rely on most of the Negroes and poor whites in their parishes. The white, Protestant farmers of the northern piney woods by contrast were a perennially discontented minority, who gave the independent Democrats, Populists and Socialists in turn their strongest support within the state. In several states, there is a conflict between a downstate metropolis and the upstate farmers. In Louisiana, that conflict was accentuated by religious and racial differences, poverty, and the high proportion of Negroes.[11]

This governing class was colloquially known as the Bourbons, taking the same name as the conservative and eastern wing of the Democratic party with whom they had much in common. They were a mixed group drawn from Confederate leaders, old planting families, and new capitalists, and resembled the Carpetbag governments in their use of a corruptible Negro vote and their acceptance of Whiggish principles of state aid to business. This was not their avowed role. The usual political oration began with an almost ritual statement of the shame of the era of Reconstruction from which the people had been rescued, and the need to loyally support the leadership against Henry Clay Warmoth, governor from 1868 to 1872, and his colored and Scallawag minions. At the same time, the Bourbons in fact secured, or local zeal procured a large part of the colored vote. The danger was that in time of great stress, the necessary intimidation and bribery would become too bare-faced and expensive. By the 1890's, that time was fast approaching.[12]

As far as the national Republican party was concerned, the Mugwump element favored the reunion of the sections and good government. Southerners should be permitted to settle the suffrage question in their own way, provided no violence was done to the constitution. One of the advantages of the Australian

---

[11] C. Vann Woodward, *Origins of the New South* (Baton Rouge, 1951), *passim;* United States Bureau of the Census, *Thirteenth Census of the United States: 1910. Abstract with Supplement for Louisiana* (Washington, 1913), 245, 569–70, 606, 610; Perry Howard, *Political Tendencies in Louisiana, 1812–1952* (Baton Rouge, 1957), figs. 23, 30, 33; Grady McWhinney, "Louisiana Socialists in the Early Twentieth Century: a Study in Rustic Radicalism," *Journal of Southern History,* XX (August, 1954), 317–19. Dr. Howard's charts indicate that the piney woods offered the strongest opposition to the Carpetbaggers in 1872 and the Bourbons in 1896–1900, mainly due to the use of the colored vote in both instances.

[12] William Mahone, leader of the Virginia Independents, contributed to a composite article on ballot reform and charged the Bourbons in his state with extensive fraud in the late elections. *North American Review,* CXLIX (December, 1889), 755–56. See also Woodward, *New South,* 96–106.

ballot, they now said, was that it ensured an orderly vote and
disfranchised illiterates, who were mostly Negro. Tennessee and
Kentucky were among the first states to adopt the reform, but
the main influence upon Wallace and the pioneers of Louisville
came from New York and its periodical press. It was rather the
tense political situation of the 1890's which forced drastic
changes in the electoral laws of the South and revealed the
mingled motives of discrimination and reform.[13]

Many of the orthodox members of the Republican party made
the South their peculiar target in the 1880's for attacking electoral abuses. Senator John J. Ingalls of Kansas in the party
campaign book of 1888 charged his opponents with a persistent
fraud which began with John Slidell's waterborne repeaters in
1844. His conclusion was bleak. The Democrats blanketed a
large area of the country with a mock election, while the North
was divided by such "false pretenses" as the antagonism between
rich and poor. The young and impetuous Theodore Roosevelt
scoffed at Cleveland's plurality in defeat and attacked the shifty
and hypocritical Mugwumps for ignoring the intimidation of
southern Republicans. Such attacks culminated in the Force
Bill introduced by his close friend, Senator Henry Cabot Lodge
of Massachusetts, in June, 1890, which sought to invoke the
fourteenth amendment and resume federal control of elections.
The move failed, giving the southern Bourbons a further issue to
exploit in their perennial task of suppressing local dissent.[14]

[13] Wigmore, "A Summary of Ballot Reform," *The Nation*, XLIX (August 29, 1889), 165; Wigmore, *Australian Ballot System*, 24, 34; E. L.
Godkin, "The Republican Party and the Negro," *Forum*, VII (May, 1889),
246–57; Bishop, "The Secret Ballot in Thirty-three States," 597; *The Nation*, XLI (July 23, 1885), 67 and L (January 23, 1890), 64. Bishop was
on the staff of Godkin's paper. In such matters, the influential James
Bryce followed Godkin. *American Commonwealth*, II, 205. The southern
states passed their Australian ballot laws as follows: Mississippi (1890),
Arkansas (1891), Tennessee (local in 1891 and still in 1910), Texas
(1892–1903), Alabama (1893), Virginia (1894), Florida (1895), Louisiana (1896), North Carolina (1909—local), South Carolina and Georgia
much later.

[14] Ingalls, "A Fair Vote and an Honest Count," in Long ed., *Republican
Party*, 323–38; Hagedorn ed., *Works of Theodore Roosevelt*, XIV, 81–87;

The Australian Ballot:

The sense of mission of the Populist party and their nostrums of free silver, an income tax, and public ownership of utilities attracted wide support in Louisiana and throughout the distressed South and West. The state Alliance sent delegates to the Cincinnati convention where the party was formed in May, 1891, and in the following year a ticket was entered for the state elections. However, the election was dominated by the fierce struggle over the re-charter of the extraordinarily successful Louisiana lottery, which introduced a great deal of money into the contest and split the major parties. The Populist candidate obtained only one-eighteenth of the total votes cast for governor. But in 1894, cotton dropped to less than five cents a pound, indicating the severity of the depression. The reduction of the sugar duty in the Wilson tariff was resented. In New Orleans where several corrupt councilmen were under indictment, a Citizens League was formed to back a reform candidate for mayor and a legislative ticket. A bitter struggle loomed ahead for 1896.[15]

The Populists endorsed Protection and the Republican candidate for governor, J. N. Pharr, a sugar planter. The Democrats renominated Governor Murphy J. Foster, hero of the fight against the lottery, and endorsed sound money. The Democratic-Populist fusion behind William Jennings Bryan and free silver for the presidential elections later in the year was to confuse the situation more than a little. The Bourbon speakers as usual invoked the gratitude of a redeemed Louisiana and drew attention to the motley array in opposition—"scallawag, carpet-bagger, negro, sugar planter and populist, all lying together in one common political bed." Pharr's defense of the colored people and his warning to his followers to be prepared to face violence on

---

Woodward, *New South,* 254–55. The Plaquemine frauds, organized by John Slidell, probably assured Polk of his majority in Louisiana. For an example of a congressional investigation with a separate minority report, see *Senate Reports,* 48 Cong., 1 sess., 512, which deals with an election in 1884 in a Mississippi county with a Negro majority.

15 *Report of the Secretary of State* (Baton Rouge, 1892) ; Lucia Elizabeth Daniel, "The Louisiana People's Party," *Louisiana Historical Quarterly,* XXVI (October, 1943), 1055–1149.

election day drew a note of grim scorn. He seemed to concentrate on a protective tariff and a fair count and placed responsibility for both on the shoulders of the southern whites. The tariff had been the policy of John C. Calhoun and Judah P. Benjamin; and if the Negro was ignorant and purchasable, he said, this stream could rise no higher than its source. He was able to fill a large meeting hall in New Orleans in which half the audience was colored.[16]

There were three tickets in the city, as the white button of the Citizens League vied enthusiastically with the red rooster of the Regulars. The League emphasized that their primary aim was good government for the city and a fair count, and they later decided to print both Democratic and Republican state tickets. This won them the endorsement of a large meeting of colored voters, and on April 7, a parish Republican convention anxiously debated the issue. The climax of this meeting came when Henry Clay Warmoth, the Reconstruction governor of Louisiana from 1868 to 1872, and a veritable king among Carpetbaggers, mounted a table and cried, "Three cheers for the Citizen's League." It was not quite twenty-two years since the race riots in the city. The wheel had turned full circle.[17]

The League organized armed watchers and obtained an orderly vote in New Orleans, but snippets in the press suggest a confused and disorderly election in many other parishes. Boxes mysteriously disappeared and the bewildered colored voters were rejected or welcomed according to the disposition of the local party managers. Sixteen days before the election, it was announced that state troops had been ordered to Opelousas to check further outbreaks of violence. Two hundred armed and mounted men were said to be lying outside the town ready to swoop down on the court-

[16] New Orleans *Daily Picayune,* March 4, March 15, 1896. Louisiana later sent a free silver delegation to the national convention. The New Orleans *Times-Democrat* and other papers supported Bryan, but the *Daily Picayune,* which might be described as a house journal of the state Mugwumps, continued its strong opposition to free silver and endorsed the National Democratic ticket. It drew grim comfort from the result. June 15, November 4, 1896.

[17] New Orleans *Daily Picayune,* March 24, April 2, 3, 8, 9, 1896.

house. Many Negroes had renounced their vote and were taking refuge in the town to escape further punishment, while white sympathizers were planning countermeasures. In this tense situation, the sheriff was nowhere to be found. Election day was marred by a fatal shooting and Pharr's ticket narrowly carried the parish. The result was as follows:

	House	Senate
Democrats	67	30
Republicans	9	4
Populists	16	2
Independents	6	—
	98	36	[18]

When Foster's victory was announced in the press, Pharr threw off the mask. He asserted that he was the candidate of white supremacy, for the Democrats could not have won without huge and fraudulent majorities in the black-majority parishes along the river valleys. Significantly, the attendance of Negroes was only a fraction of those at his previous meetings in New Orleans. The city press reluctantly conceded his claims. Only the Australian ballot and amendment of the constitution could save Louisiana for the Democracy, warned the *Times-Democrat*. The Fusion committee then formally demanded that the legislature examine the returns and tally sheets in detail and called on white men to assemble in Baton Rouge when the session began on May 11. In this tense situation, the Citizens League could act as mediators. Walter Flower, their successful candidate for mayor, had doubled Foster's majority in the city, and their team in the new legislature of twenty-three in the House and nine in the Senate could hold a balance of power against regular Democrats from the rest of the state. Charles Janvier, president of the League, met the governor and Pharr, who finally agreed that the returns be referred to the proper committee of the legislature, and that laws be passed to provide for the Australian ballot and a constitutional convention to examine the whole suffrage question. On May 14, the two houses

[18] *Ibid.*, April 5, 15, 19, 21–26, 1896; *Report of the Secretary of State* (Baton Rouge, 1896).

in general assembly refused to go behind the returns and by a vote of eighty-six to forty-eight, declared Foster elected by 116,216 votes to 90,138 for Pharr. The League provided speakers for both sides, and enabled the Fusion to save something from the debacle by having Pharr's protest read into the official record.[19]

On May 22, Henry Bruns of the League released a draft of the Australian ballot law based on the model law of Massachusetts. Its application was limited to cities with a population over fifty thousand, that is to New Orleans. Support mounted. The agrarian radicals regarded the election as yet another instance of the submissive and corruptible Negro vote being used against them. Regular and reform Democrats resented their dependence upon this vote, and confessed some shame for the practices of the last election. The tension between the parties and the unseating of a Louisiana congressman early in the campaign was making the situation too difficult to handle. Why not end it and almost eliminate the Negro vote by legal means? The Australian ballot would provide a swift and partial solution until a constitutional convention could be called with all due preparation and solemnity.[20]

The Democratic caucus accepted a state-wide election reform bill which was introduced into the House on June 19. That same day, the press reported that the Republican national convention had nominated William McKinley and adopted a platform which prominently featured sound money and a sugar duty. This would strengthen the hand of the party in New Orleans and southern Louisiana. At the same time, there was mounting suspicion among Populists, Republicans and reform Democrats of the sudden conversion of the Bourbons and their convention proposals, which

[19] New Orleans *Daily Picayune,* May 1, 2, 6–8, 15, 1896; New Orleans *Times-Democrat,* April 25, 1896; Sidney James Romero, "The Political Career of Murphy James Foster, Governor of Louisiana, 1892–1900," *Louisiana Historical Quarterly,* XXVIII (October, 1945), 1179–83. The terms are as announced to the Citizens League assemblymen by Janvier.

[20] Howard, *Political Tendencies,* 100–01; Daniel, "The Louisiana People's Party," 1111; Woodward, *New South,* 79–82, 321–49; New Orleans *Times-Democrat,* March 16, 20, April 25, 26, 1896; New Orleans *Daily Picayune,* May 22, 1896.

envisaged a limited list of subjects and no popular ratification of the constitution. As the Fusion had polled so heavily, some Democratic leaders now feared that the Republicans could possibly carry the presidential election and later the elections to the convention. They might even persuade the Citizens League to concentrate on their proposed city charter bill rather than a convention. Governor Foster leaped into the fray to urge the full support of his party for the Australian ballot and the "prohibitive" convention laws. Though once doubtful, he felt that a measure adopted by three-quarters of the states could at least be tried. In effect, he was using the ballot to conciliate the League and make a wedge for his convention bill. After some skirmishing by the Republicans, the Australian ballot law passed the House on June 29 by fifty-five votes to twenty-seven, and then the Senate by twenty-three to nine. The minority in the House included all sixteen Populists and four of the nine Republicans; and in the Senate, included both Populists and three of the four Republicans. The League did not fail in their other objectives and secured a new charter for the city with a civil service commission and a port commission.[21]

In the same session which met in the shadow of party warfare and passed such vital reforms as the Australian ballot and a civil service law, the legislators did not fail to protect the virtue of the citizens. Tersely and without qualification, as doth befit a righteous spirit, they passed laws prohibiting gambling with dice for money, and the wearing of hats in theaters.[22]

The combined effect of the Australian ballot and a Democratic-

[21] New Orleans *Daily Picayune*, June 16, 19, 20, 25, 30, July 1, 2, 10, 1896; New Orleans *Times-Democrat*, July 1, 1896, for criticism of the convention bill; *Acts Passed by the General Assembly* (Baton Rouge, 1896), Nos. 45, 52, 70, 137. The latter is the Australian ballot law. The Populists voted against it, although their press favored the Australian ballot and disfranchisement in June, 1896. As American states, unlike the Australian, have no Hansard record of the debates in the legislature, and as the press accounts are so sketchy, some doubts must remain. I have tried to clarify this tricky point and am most grateful to Dr. Henry Dethloff of the University of Southwestern Louisiana for his comments and for forwarding a copy of his unpublished paper, "Populism and Reform in Louisiana" (1967).

[22] *Acts*, 1896, Nos. 22, 62.

Populist fusion led to an unusually quiet election in November, 1896. The *Daily Picayune,* which had backed the National Democratic ticket, was pleased to find its judgment confirmed on both the political situation and the manner of the election. Some Republicans in New Orleans complained that the provisions of the new registration law seemed open to confusion when their supporters were involved; but the rosy prospect of empty desks at the customs house and post office speedily dispelled their worries. The first phase was now complete. As the *Daily Picayune* clearly put it: "The election bill is necessary to insure fair and honest elections under the present suffrage qualifications, and it should become a law as a measure preparatory to the revision of the suffrage provisions in the Constitution."[23]

"Get rid of the illiterate and corrupt voters and assure control of Louisiana by the whites," said the *Times-Democrat* on February 7, 1898, the day before the constitutional convention opened with this as its major purpose. The delegates simply regarded the colored vote as the same thing as the corruptible vote; but the fourteenth and fifteenth amendments did not permit direct disfranchisement. Many of the delegates clearly rejected the warnings of southern Mugwump reformers that they should not try to enfranchise every white male, so ingenious solutions were needed. The president of the convention expressed the common racialist sentiments of the meeting when he declaimed: first, "The problem which we desire to solve is to undo the greatest crime of the nineteenth century—the placing of the ballot in the hands of the negro race by the Fifteenth amendment to the Constitution of the United States. . . ." and second, that he would not disfranchise those who had stood by him during the race riots of September, 1874. A delegate from Iberia parish urged that they respect Cajun customs and ensure a vote for their illiterates. To some, the Negro was even more suspect when educated. Louisiana, like the other southern states, introduced a literacy and property qualification for the suffrage, and as an alternative for poor and illiterate

[23] New Orleans *Daily Picayune,* June 23, November 4, 1896; New Orleans *Times-Democrat,* November 6, 1896.

whites, the law allowed the son or grandson of a person qualified at January 1, 1867 to himself qualify. This was the "grandfather clause," Louisiana's famous gift to political science. Her senators at once pronounced it illegal, but it lasted until 1915 when the Supreme Court delivered a similar opinion, for a Negro was ipso facto barred at the given date.[24]

Delegates mainly criticized the poll tax. It was possible to be robbed of a vote, but they said it was undemocratic to have to purchase it. The tax was adopted, but its operation suspended until 1900. The further reform of the compulsory direct primary in 1906, like the Australian ballot a nation-wide reform due to the same mingling of motives, helped further to decrease voter turnout and concern. For as the party was a private association, the reduced Negro vote could be eliminated entirely in the face of a united front after the primary campaign. As far as the machine was concerned, the nomination process simply went back a stage further. Thus in 1897, there were 294,432 registered voters, of whom 164,088 were white and 130,344 were Negro. By 1900, the voters had decreased to 130,757, of whom only 5,320 were Negroes. The number of white voters had also been reduced, and the turnout at the gubernatorial election had declined from about seventy percent to fifty-eight percent. The introduction of the poll tax further reduced the voters to 117,993 people in 1910, only 730 of whom were Negroes, although according to the United States census, there were 414,919 males over the age of twenty-one in the state, of whom 240,001 were white and 174,211 colored. The turnout was alarmingly small. There was no general election in 1908, and less than fifty-seven thousand voted in the general elections of 1904 and 1912.[25]

The party leaders not only reduced the electorate in 1898, but amended the Australian ballot law to permit easier manipulation of the electors remaining. They introduced the Indiana system

[24] New Orleans *Times-Democrat*, February 7, 9, 10, March 4, 18, 1898; *Guinn v. United States*, 238 U.S. 347 (1915).

[25] *Report of the Secretary of State* (Baton Rouge, 1898, 1900, 1904, 1908, 1912); Bureau of the Census, *Thirteenth Census . . . Louisiana*, 605; *Acts*, 1906, No. 49.

whereby the candidates were grouped in a party column under a distinctive emblem with a special and easy method of voting a straight ticket.

When John Parker of the Good Government League and the national Progressive party entered the general election in 1916, responsible opinion said openly that it was the first real campaign since 1896 and would give the voters some sadly needed political education. The turnout was about one hundred twenty-nine thousand, or more than double that of 1912. However, the campaign tended to degenerate into an unreal and typical contest between "bossdom" and "blackdom," in which the reformers raised the dread specter of boss rule, and the regulars replied that all whites must stand firm to avoid the return of the Carpetbaggers.[26]

Apathy did not mean clean elections. This Good Government League had been organized in 1910 to secure a commission form of government for New Orleans and to nominate a gubernatorial candidate for the primary. The campaign became a veritable crusade against the bosses of the Choctaw Club which controlled the party machine in the city and slogans such as "Vote for Hall and redeem Louisiana" echoed the contests of a generation or two before. After a year's work, fourteen to fifteen thousand names were removed from the roll by checking the "cemetery and hobo vote of the ring." Large advertisements offered cash rewards for information of violence or illegal assistance at the polls. Luther Hall was elected governor; but the machine carried the city comfortably and repeated the dose when the people later voted for the small council under the new charter. Some members of the League were amazed. Like bosses elsewhere, the Club was demonstrating that it had the political power and skills to withstand an emotional tirade or mere tinkering with the machinery of government.[27]

Louisiana politics thus consisted of a series of tepid and trivial

[26] New Orleans *Times-Picayune,* April 8, 19, 1916. The two papers cited frequently in this chapter merged in 1915.

[27] New Orleans *Times-Democrat,* January 2, 8, 21–23, 1912; *Report of the Secretary of State* (Baton Rouge, 1912).

campaigns, enlivened by the occasional crusade of the holy "outs" against the corrupt "ins," with the bosses and Negroes as stock villains. Meanwhile, the essential needs of progress and welfare were often ignored in the public forum. The limited outlook of the reformers was helping to make it so. The Australian ballot in Louisiana was helping to strangle responsible politics in the state from inanition and apathy. No Republican or third-party representatives sat in the legislature between 1898 and 1964. The blurred distinction between the factions gathered within the one party was only occasionally clarified at the presidential elections, or in the meteoric rise and fall of a Huey Long.

By 1944, when the all-white primary was held unconstitutional, a few Negro voters were being enrolled by one of the rival factions. Progress was slow. In 1960, one-third of those registered were in three parishes, and the proportion of white to Negro voters was six to one, but their proportion in the population was about two to one. The breathless change of recent years is another story. The prospect of reapportionment of electorates, the Voting Rights Act of 1965, the Republican resurgence in the South, and urban and economic growth are breaking up the old sectional bonds and characteristics. Perhaps, before long, a chapter such as this will be unnecessary.[28]

[28] For the progress but relative poverty of Louisiana in the Progressive era, see Bureau of the Census, *Thirteenth Census . . . Louisiana*, 276, 438, 653. See also *Smith v. Allwright*, 321 U.S. 649 (1944); recent reports of the Secretary of State; *Revised Statutes*, 7 vols. and supplement (Baton Rouge, 1950), II, title 18: Elections.

CHAPTER V

The Opening of a Road

The ballot-reform movement promises to have effects far wider than the mere achievement of a single reform. It is the opening of a road (perhaps the only road) to the whole field of political improvements.

(John H. Wigmore, 1889)

The hand-writing in the ballot booth is the hand-writing on the wall to our municipal Belshazzars.

(Alfred B. Mason, 1894)

It is neither seemly nor safe to hint that the government of the largest city in the States is a despotism of the alien by the alien for the alien, tempered with occasional insurrections of the decent folk.

(Rudyard Kipling, 1892)[1]

The presidential election of 1892 offered an extraordinary contrast with the previous contest. There seemed to be more factual argument and fewer noisy processions, and the day itself was generally quiet and orderly. The same candidates were running, Benjamin Harrison and Grover Cleveland, two solid citizens well known and widely respected, but this may not have restrained partisan zeal at the ward level. The McKinley tariff offered the voters a clear-cut issue. The admission of new states and the entry of the Populist party created uncertainty for the party managers. But the most obvious explanation of the change was the adoption in the interval of the Australian ballot in thirty-eight states. The *Nation,* which had long supported Cleveland

[1] Wigmore, *Australian Ballot System,* 56; Alfred Bishop Mason, "How to Bring Public Sentiment to Bear upon the Choice of Good Public Officials: Through the Primaries," *Proceedings of the First National Conference for Good City Government* (Philadelphia, 1894), 186; Rudyard Kipling, *Letters of Travel, 1892–1913, and Other Sketches,* in *Works of Rudyard Kipling,* 31 vols. (London, 1913–18), XXVII, 14–16.

and ballot reform, was naturally pleased and eager for more. As large expenditures to get out the vote were no longer required, it urged the states to copy the British Corrupt Practices Act of 1883 and strictly limit them.[2]

The election of 1896 was also well conducted despite a heated campaign in which some eastern newspapers had described the Democratic candidate, William Jennings Bryan, as a kind of wild-eyed anarchist, while some Populist speakers pulled all the stops out in denouncing the bankers. Most people assumed that the voting would be secret and fair. The press reminded the national party chairmen, who had been arguing before the election about the coercion of the labor vote by employers, that the charge was now irrelevant. Whereas the Republican victory of 1888 had been freely ascribed to "blocks of five" and colonization of voters, the present result was described, regretfully or joyfully, as a vote for prosperity and sound money.[3]

In some cities, the Australian ballot manifestly failed to achieve its purpose. Chicago and Cook County continued to enhance their reputation for a hearty indifference to electoral reform. The World's Fair of 1893 greatly increased the rewards obtainable in the Levee or "sporting district," and envious eyes were cast on the control wielded in the first ward by two accomplished saloon-keepers and ward heelers, "Bathhouse" John Coghlan and "Hinky-dink" Kenna. The aldermanic elections of April, 1894, left a bloody trail of two shot dead and over two score injured. "Gambler Bill" Skakel, running as an independent and a Republican, stood no chance. The police appeared at intervals only to cart off the bodies, usually battered Skakel voters and watchers. The police were also in danger, for in the second ward a red-haired Irishman named Jim McGinn knocked down three members of the force, as well as sundry voters. To reinforce the thugs, the machine had assembled a large team of hirelings to repeat, personate, and otherwise exploit a defective roll. The only alternative to elec-

2 *The Nation,* LIV (June 16, 1892), 442, LV (November 17, 1892), 361, 368; *Public Opinion,* November 12, 19, 1892.
3 *Public Opinion,* October 29, November 12, 1896.

toral service for many of the unemployed in this year was to join Coxey's army.[4]

As Coghlan ran ahead of the Democratic mayor in several precincts despite the opposition within the party, it was almost certain that his faction had stuffed the boxes. This was not the kind of election intended by the reformers of 1891. The Chicago *Daily Tribune* delivered the crowning insult: "The re-election of John Coghlan was secured in the first ward by methods which would disgrace the river parishes of Louisiana."[5]

Bribery, as well as intimidation, still persisted, The New York law was unsatisfactory until 1895, when the paster or party ballots were abolished. In some precincts, party workers exploited the provision for assisting the illiterate and disabled and continued the old traffic in ballots. Many voters were still purchasable, whether the old Yankee farmers of Rhode Island, Connecticut and Delaware, or the immigrant Italian miners of Pennsylvania.[6]

An effective Australian ballot law usually checked such obvious abuses. But as time passed, several observers pointed out that it did not seriously weaken the power of the machine, despite the predictions of Ivins and other reformers. The boss no longer controlled the nominations and no longer had an excuse to levy assessments; but the law recognized the parties and deliberately obstructed the independent candidates. The spirit of party loyalty remained strong and the voter accepted the ticket ranged down

---

[4] Chicago *Daily Tribune,* April 2–5, 1894. The paper had warned of the defective rolls when the ballot law was being discussed. *Ibid.,* January 4, 1891. The first ward was not typical. The Republicans exploited the crusade against vice launched by the English journalist, W. T. Stead, and took twenty-two of the thirty-four aldermanic seats.

[5] *Ibid.,* April 5, 1894.

[6] Jeremiah W. Jenks, "Money in Practical Politics," *Century Illustrated Monthly Magazine,* XLIV (October, 1892), 948–52; McCook, "The Alarming Proportion of Venal Voters," 1–13; George Kennan, "Holding up a State," *Outlook,* LXIII (February 7, 14, 21, 1903), 277–83, 386–92, 429–36; James Woodburn, *Political Parties and Party Problems in the United States* (New York, 1924), 401–02. Connecticut and Rhode Island passed their ballot laws in 1889, and Delaware, the subject of Kennan's articles, in 1891.

the long party column, which was furnished for him by the continuing machine. The boss was still an intermediary between the "needy rich and the grateful poor"—to use the phrase of the New York reformer, Richard Welling—the one anxious for favors and franchises, and the other ready to obey the agent who attended to a mass of petty needs at a time of rapid immigration and rudimentary social services. The boss and especially the precinct leader in a large city was always ready to attend a funeral or a wedding feast, to furnish a basket of food to a widow or to bail out her unruly son. Few contemporaries seemed to realize the implications of his busy and varied life. Theodore Roosevelt was one of the few well-educated, middle-class reformers to do so. At an early date, he discerned the sources and results of the boss's power. In an article written in 1886, he concluded:

> Ordinary citizens, to whom participation in politics is merely a disagreeable duty, will always be beaten by the organized array of politicians to whom it is both duty, business, and pleasure, and who are knit together and to outsiders by their social relations.[7]

Some dissatisfied reformers chose to be sarcastic. Delos F. Wilcox, holder of the Ph.D. from Columbia University, a public official, and writer on municipal subjects, wrote in 1912 in a manner that was becoming increasingly common:

> As a last means of civic education we have the widely-heralded ballot box and voting machine. It cannot be denied that the successful manipulation of an average American ballot is a mechanical invention of which the electorate may justly feel proud. To mark it without voiding it is something. To fold it is also something. To sign your name to the roll proves that you can write. To tell the clerks every time you

[7] M. Ostrogorski, *Democracy and the Organisation of Political Parties*, 2 vols. (New York, 1902), II, 346–50, 500–07; Richard W. Welling, *As the Twig is Bent* (New York, 1942), Preface, 57–65; Robert C. Brooks, *Corruption in American Politics and Life* (New York, 1910), 22–25; Theodore Roosevelt, "Machine Politics in New York City," in Hagedorn ed., *Works of Theodore Roosevelt*, XIII, 98; Roosevelt, *Autobiography*, 96–97, 162–66. Roosevelt's article appeared in the *Century* in November, 1886.

register when you were born, where you voted last and how long you have lived at your present address, keeps the memory of your past history green. To be able to pull the levers of a complex mechanical apparatus and make it cast your vote is, indeed, a badge of civic distinction. But the finest educational product of the election process comes with the ability to vote a split ticket. How pitiful it is that the educational value of the ballot should so largely consist in learning this difficult sleight of hand.[8]

Others pressed for further reform to rectify this situation by analogy with the Australian ballot or deduction from democratic theory. The most complete catalog was known as the Oregon system. In this state the Australian ballot law passed in 1891 began a sequence of reforms between 1891 and 1910 which included a registration law; the Initiative and Referendum; the Direct Primary; a Corrupt Practices Act; an amendment binding the legislature to the popular choice of United States Senator; recall of officials; a presidential pre-convention primary; and an Employers Liability Act. The Initiative law, though much admired, led to unexpected problems. There had been at least one notorious case of petition-hunting for blackmail purposes, and a group of inveterate petitioners could become a "rival legislature."[9]

Such a sequence of reforms spans the two movements usually described as Populism and Progressivism, and reveals a continuing inheritance from the era of civil service reform, the Mugwump bolt, and the Australian ballot. The usual textbook suggests the latter stopped short in 1884, thus leaving a sufficient gap before presenting the 1890's as a kind of unusual and self-contained decade in which Free Silver, the Pullman Strike and the Cuban war came and went. Progressivism then blazed forth as something new about 1900 conveniently close to the unexpected advent of Theodore Roosevelt to the White House. This arrangement is not basically wrong, but the emphasis is stereotyped and misguided. A reform

[8] Delos F. Wilcox, *Government by all the People: or the Initiative, Referendum and Recall as Instruments of Democracy* (New York, 1912), 277–78.

[9] Allen H. Eaton, *The Oregon System: the Story of Direct Legislation in Oregon* (Chicago, 1912), 48–49, 159.

such as the Australian ballot required attention over a long period, and was shared by different groups in common. There were strong resemblances between Mugwumps and Progressives as a social type. Nevertheless, the terms are useful to designate groups and periods. The Mugwump spirit flourished in an era devoted to raw growth, whether in wheat, steel or million-dollar incomes, and expressed a distaste for the coarseness and corruption resulting from such growth while sharing the laissez-faire assumptions of the apostles of growth and corporate organization. Populism was essentially the last wave of radical, agrarian protest which followed the Civil War. The embattled yeomen of the plains blew hot and cold demanding free silver and stay laws in 1896, and when prices improved lost interest in regulating the economy and voted their normal Republican ticket in 1900. The southern Populist diverted his energies to spelling out the details of segregation. Progressivism was less sectional and limited than Populism, but more varied in expression than Mugwump reform. It was a nationwide wave of reform, more sophisticated, urban, and middle class in its drive and appeal. It sprang from the older individualist values and from the naive but determined belief that the plain man was an honest but thwarted elector and entrepreneur. Deep down he wanted good government, and if one mechanism failed, then the Progressives felt that by further tinkering the people would be able to act and force their rulers to respond. As Charles A. Beard wrote in 1912: "Nearly all of the proposals designed to checkmate legislative abuses have been based upon the assumption that the hope for better government lay in *more* democracy rather than less." Some measures were novel such as the commission form of government in cities; others were carried over from the Populists such as the direct election of United States Senators which first appeared in their platform in 1892 and was not finally adopted until the passage of the Seventeenth Amendment in 1913. Both Mugwump and Populist supported the Australian ballot, and the Progressives were eager to spell out further installments of electoral reform and denounce the ubiquitous Boss. Lincoln Steffens, the muckraking journalist; Tom Johnson, reform mayor of Cleveland; Albert J. Beveridge, advocate of Imperialism and pure food laws; Hiram Johnson, who promised to kick the Southern Pacific out of California politics; Robert LaFollette, champion of the direct primary and equal taxation laws in Wisconsin; Theodore Roosevelt, "trust-buster" and conservationist; and Woodrow Wilson, eloquent spokesman of the New Freedom—these men are of the essence of the Progressive movement.[10]

A reformer might set out his case as follows. Where a people believed in representative democracy and manhood suffrage, they should pass detailed laws to ensure that the legislature provided an accurate expression of the popular will. The parties could not now offer the excuse that it was expensive to print and peddle their tickets. Most states had registration laws and the Australian ballot. They should now define and prohibit corrupt practices as in Britain, and adopt a direct primary, a compulsory vote, and a short ballot.[11]

Ivins and Dana had referred to the British Ballot Act of 1872 and the Corrupt Practices Act of 1883 almost in the same breath. The *Century* and the *Nation* urged this next step after the successful trial of the new ballot in elections from 1889 to 1892. A bill was first presented in Massachusetts in 1889 but defeated in the upper house. Gradually the problem was taken in hand. By 1908, twenty states had passed laws requiring the filing of campaign expenditures, and some, much stricter than others, specified the items and maxima allowed. In his annual message of December, 1907, President Roosevelt made the startling suggestion that Congress pay the legitimate expenses of the major parties, providing there was a limit on individual donations. Such a law failed in Washington, but was passed in Colorado in 1909. However, the national chairmen voluntarily accepted the spirit of such a sugges-

[10] Samuel P. Hays, *The Response to Industrialism, 1885–1914* (Chicago, 1957), 24–27; Richard Hofstadter, *The Age of Reform: from Bryan to F. D. R.* (New York, 1956), 5, 131; Charles A. Beard and Birl E. Shultz eds., *Documents on the State-wide Initiative, Referendum and Recall* (New York, 1912), 12. Italics are in the original. The quotation comes from Beard's interesting introduction.

[11] Seymour and Frary, *How the World Votes*, II, 315.

tion to curb lavish campaign expenditures and in 1908 publicly disclosed the major contributions.[12]

As the Australian ballot was designed to provide a cheaper and purer election, some argued that a compulsory vote was a necessary corollary. It would spread printing costs, check personation, and encourage public spirit. Colonial Virginia had passed such a law in 1705 but it had fallen into disuse. The first serious advocate in more modern times seems to have been a Baltimore lawyer, Harris J. Chilton in 1882. He sent a draft bill to the *North American Review* in December, 1887, as an addendum to the ballot reform bill drafted by the editor, Allen Thorndike Rice. A bill was narrowly defeated in Massachusetts and proposed in New York and Maryland. After that, the proposal seemed to stop dead. Compulsory voting is now a feature of Australian elections. It was first adopted in Queensland in 1915 and for Commonwealth elections in 1924, but the age of borrowing is probably over.[13]

The representative principle was endangered not only by the low voter turnout, but also by a split among the greater number of candidates encouraged by the new system. Daniel Remsen pointed out in 1896 that the governors in seventeen states had been elected by less than half the votes cast. He urged an inno-

---

[12] Editorial, "Further Electoral Reform," *Century Illustrated Monthly Magazine*, XXXIX (February, 1890), 633; Dana, "The Practical Working of the Australian System of Voting in Massachusetts," 739; Brooks, *Corruption in American Politics*, 221–30. Dana said that the law would be ineffective until a defeated candidate could unseat a victor as in Britain. Dana to S. W. McCall, January 1, 1894, Dana Papers.

[13] Harris J. Clinton, "Compulsory Voting Demanded," *North American Review*, CXLV (December, 1887), 685–86; Frederick W. Holls, "Compulsory Voting," *Annals of the American Academy of Political and Social Science*, I (April, 1891), 586–614. I am grateful to Miss Geneva Kebler of the Michigan Historical Commission, Lansing, for furnishing the photostat of a letter from Harris J. Chilton, the name on the letterhead and presumably the author, to Governor Cyrus Luce, dated July 1, 1889, who had urged the Australian ballot in his message of that year. Chilton said that he had urged the reform for the past seven years, including publication of an article in the *North American Review*, as an addendum to the Australian system of voting. The only reference I can find is the brief article cited above.

vation first adopted by Queensland in August, 1892, and now another feature of Australian elections. He called it the "automatic fusion," although it is now usually called preferential voting, as distinct from the British system of "first past the post" or victory by plurality. Voters number all the candidates in consecutive order, and if none has an absolute majority, the lowest is struck out and his second preferences distributed. It is simpler and cheaper than holding a runoff election if an absolute majority is required. Naturally it is more cumbersome with a blanket ballot, but such a bill was presented in New York in 1896, and the sample ballot used for demonstration showed a second blank square permitting a second choice opposite each single-office candidate on the ballot.[14]

The Short Ballot movement established a flourishing national organization in 1910 with Governor Woodrow Wilson of New Jersey, former professor and president of Princeton, as president, and twenty-eight-year-old Richard S. Childs of New York as a tireless publicist and part-time secretary. Mr. Childs first introduced his proposal in an article in the *Outlook* in July, 1909. A donation from his father and a favorable response from the mail enabled him to proceed. One of the first to respond was Arthur Ludington, formerly of Princeton and then compiling his invaluable digest of ballot laws, and he in turn introduced governor-elect Wilson. They believed that a voter could not exercise a responsible choice when confronted with a huge, blanket ballot and a host of labels and names. The ballot should be confined to a few important offices, and the remainder should be appointed or absorbed within the civil service. Similarly, cities should adopt the commission form of government, in which a small, nonpartisan team were elected by the whole city and given wide powers. Thereby the informed citizen would again come into his own. Such in brief were their views, and late in 1912, they claimed ten thousand three hundred members and more than two hundred cities

[14] Daniel Remsen, "The Fusion of Political Parties," *Annals of the American Academy of Political and Social Science*, VIII (July, 1896), 32–49.

which had adopted the commission form. The Short Ballot was on the platform of the Progressive party, and endorsed by eleven governors. However, the results were meager. The *Short Ballot Bulletin,* which had begun in February, 1911, was absorbed by the *National Municipal Review* in 1920, the organ of the National Municipal League, and Mr. Childs, a former president, has been chairman of the executive committee of the League since 1947.[15]

In the past, English visitors had scornfully suggested that civic improvement depended upon basic political reforms. The population of greater New York, as created in 1898, had doubled in twenty years. To the acid-tongued Sir Lepel Griffin of the Indian civil service, and to Rudyard Kipling, a literary celebrity of twenty-seven with an American wife, the city presented a slovenly and heedless appearance under slovenly and heedless boss rule. Kipling described her crowded and ill-paved streets as "kin to the approaches of a Zulu kraal," and her government as "a despotism of the alien by the alien for the alien, tempered with occasional insurrections of the decent folk." The caddish Sir Lepel sneered at her police and American women by turns. In his classic survey, the English scholar James Bryce described municipal government as the one notable failure of the American Commonwealth and used the corruption and greed of Tammany Hall and the Tweed Ring in New York for extensive illustration.[16]

Such criticism was not unheeded. The National Municipal League was established by the first National Conference for Good City Government, which was attended by many well-known reformers at Philadelphia in January, 1894. The main initiative was

[15] Edna Bullock ed., *Short Ballot* (New York, 1915); Richard S. Childs, *Civic Victories: the Story of an Unfinished Revolution* (New York, 1952), 83–91; Richard S. Childs to the author, January 30, September 8, 1963. The Bullock bibliography of 156 items is dominated by Mr. Childs's contributions, with Charles A. Beard probably running second. By 1919, he felt that the movement had run its course and he should turn his attention to the National Municipal League.

[16] Sir Lepel Henry Griffin, *The Great Republic* (New York, 1884), 48–61, 115; Kipling, *Letters of Travel*, 13–18; Bryce, *American Commonwealth,* I, 640–79.

taken by the City Club and Good Government clubs of New York City. The League, which still flourishes, was therefore active before and after the conventional limits of the Progressive era. Proposals were presented by the older generation of reformers which would later become hallmarks of Progressivism. At the first conference, Alfred B. Mason of New York presented a paper urging compulsory primary elections as a corollary to the Australian ballot. The boss once said, "vote as you please as long as I count"; now he was saying, "vote as you please as long as I choose the candidates." Mason claimed that a primary would secure better officials and drive out the boss. The first direct primary law was passed in Wisconsin in 1903 during the term of Governor Robert LaFollette, and all states but four had followed suit by 1917. The older reform had recognized political parties for the first time as institutions of the state for providing candidates for the elections. By the new reform, the state was now regulating the parties' organization and membership.[17]

Other well-known reforms were the Initiative, Referendum and Recall. The Initiative permitted a group of voters—eight percent in Oregon—to petition that a proposed law or constitutional amendment be placed on the ballot at the next general election for the voters to accept or reject. The other two permitted by petition a referendum before a law was put into effect, and a referendum on a proposal to recall officials. Supporters claimed that it strengthened representative government by encouraging the informed citizen and allowing him to keep a check upon the parties and the legislature. First adopted by South Dakota in 1898, the state-wide Initiative and Referendum had been adopted by 1911 in twelve states and proposed or partially adopted in ten others. Oregon had been the first to include constitutional amendments in the Initiative, and in 1908 added the Recall. These reforms were championed by the new Progressive party, and by Delos F. Wilcox,

[17] Mason, "How to Bring Public Sentiment to Bear . . . ," 186–90. He preferred to elect delegates to a nominating convention rather than adopt the New Jersey plan, which anticipated the direct election of party nominees now in use.

Charles A. Beard, and Ellis P. Oberholtzer among the political scientists.[18]

The Oregon experience suggested that the system was being used to excess. In four elections, sixty-four measures were put up, forty-eight by the Initiative and sixteen by the legislature, of which thirty-one were accepted and thirty-three rejected. Half of this number or thirty-two were proposed in 1910 alone, when twenty-three failed. Of the nine which then passed, none obtained an absolute majority of the voters due to the heavy dropout below the gubernatorial contest on the ballot.[19]

The example of Theodore Roosevelt, and his conscious theory that the President was a "steward" of the people who should carry out his program and not remain a mere executive, encouraged various reforms designed to strengthen the government. Nineteenth-century reformers usually attacked patronage and wanted to replace it with more elective posts and an expanded civil service. As the elective ticket often helped the machine or obstructed reform, many Progressives preferred a stronger executive and legislature curbed by the short ballot and recall. Governor George Hodges of Kansas in March, 1913, made a number of interesting and specific recommendations. He wanted a unicameral legislature of only thirty members with a four- or six-year term, holding longer sessions, with the governor in the chair. He felt that the members, although subject to the recall, would gain greater efficiency and prestige. Likewise, the new school of municipal reformers wanted to consolidate authority, enlarge the powers of the mayor, and run their city as an active and nonpartisan business enterprise.[20]

[18] Eaton, *Oregon System, passim;* Bear and Shultz, *Documents,* 1–70. For Wilcox, see fn. 8. Oberholtzer, the noted historian, was at this time a journalist. He had published his dissertation on *The Referendum* in 1893, and two revised editions followed in 1900 and 1911.

[19] Eaton, *Oregon System,* 148–49.

[20] Bullock, *Short Ballot,* 66–70; Roosevelt, *Autobiography,* 389, 395; Frederic C. Howe, *The Confessions of a Reformer* (New York, 1925), 80–126, 176–81. Seth Low, reform mayor of Brooklyn between 1882 and 1885, anticipated the new approach to municipal reform in a number of published addresses and in the chapter he wrote for Bryce, *American Commonwealth,* I, 656–79, or II, 296–317 in the 1st. ed. of 1888. This again illustrates the interaction between Mugwump and Progressive reform.

The Opening of a Road

The commission form of government in the cities and a mayor who could appoint department heads for the currency of his own term in the manner of a British Prime Minister suggests a strange reform proffered by Albert M. Kales of the Northwestern University School of Law in 1914. It appeared in *Unpopular Government in the United States,* a wide-ranging polemic, but not untypical of a time when other academics such as Beard were writing extensively in favor of the Short Ballot and the Initiative-referendum. Kales's theme was that long tickets and ignorant voters were producing government by the few. His projected reforms included the Initiative-referendum; unicameral legislatures; and a commission form of government for the states. The latter was a scheme to join the legislative and executive branches. The extraordinary feature the author offers as a feasible constitutional amendment for the purpose is a form of words almost identical with section 62–64 of the Australian constitution, and without acknowledgment. The present constitution came into operation in 1901. These sections create the framework and imply the necessary usages for the adoption of Cabinet government in the British manner within a federal system.[21]

The Australian ballot and the quest for political reforms in the late-nineteenth century thus merged with the Progressive era. By 1910, twenty-two years after the amendment to the Louisville charter, it had been adopted by all states but Georgia and South Carolina. It was the veteran in a decade of constant political innovation. The time was now ripe for a thorough descriptive analysis. The task was performed by Arthur Ludington, a Yale graduate and former assistant to Woodrow Wilson. He produced several articles and his invaluable digest, *American Ballot Laws, 1888–1910,* was published in 1911 as one of the regular bulletins of the New York State University. His death in 1914 at the early age of thirty-four deprived the movement of his undoubted talents.

There was now considerable variation in the state laws. Missouri, New Jersey and the territory of New Mexico had "com-

[21] Albert M. Kales, *Unpopular Government in the United States* (Chicago, 1914), esp. 171–72.

95

promise" laws which still permitted separate party ballots. In New Jersey and New Mexico, the ballots were still distributed by the parties and could be pasted, scratched or altered in any way. Tennessee and North Carolina had laws of only limited local application. These five states and Georgia and South Carolina, seven in all, may be ignored for the purpose of comparison. Depending on the state, the voter marked his ballot to the right or to the left of the candidates' names, using a rubber stamp, ink, or an indelible or common lead pencil. Twenty-eight states, including the territory of Arizona, arranged the candidates in parallel party columns, and all but two had a simple method of voting a straight ticket. The party machines preferred the further refinement of an emblem and party circle as in Louisiana and fourteen other states which simply required one mark within the circle. These emblems varied all over the nation, perhaps the most imaginative being the Prohibition party, which used in various states a sun rising over water, a hatchet, a house and yard, a phoenix, an anchor, a fountain, and a rose. Massachusetts and twelve other states used the office block arrangement, but only a few copied *all* the features of her law—alphabetic listing under the office with party designation; a separate vote for each office; and a presidential short ballot. Or put in another way, twenty-six states using the party column arrangement and three using the office block arrangement, twenty-nine in all, encouraged a straight-ticket vote. Ludington was still worried by the specter of the Tasmanian Dodge. He advised that the ballots should have a detachable stub numbered consecutively. When handed over, the number was endorsed against the voter's name on the roll. When he returned, the number was checked against his name and number on the roll, and the stub was then detached and destroyed.[22]

The Massachusetts reformers were practical enough to realize

[22] Phillip Loring Allen, "Ballot Laws and their Working," *Political Science Quarterly*, XXI (March, 1906), 38–58; Allen, "The Multifarious Australian Ballot," *North American Review*, CXCI (May, 1910), 602–11; Arthur Ludington, "Present State of the Ballot Laws in the United States," *American Political Science Review*, III (May, 1909), 252–61.

that the Electoral College was a fiction and an independent choice of Electors was pointless. The party presidential candidates were clearly identified with their own voting squares and this was deemed to be a vote for the necessary Electors nominated by the party. However, this arrangement was used elsewhere for deliberate deception. The ballot paper issued in Maryland in 1904 listed the presidential candidate opposite a square, and below him the Electors opposite similar squares. Many people inadvertently voted for the first Elector and no other, assuming that it was a vote for all. In Florida, the names of all the Electors were run in a continuous line. The illiterates, most of whom were Negro, had to vote haphazardly, and many Populists and Socialists also threw their votes away by miscounting down the list. As a result, the first Republican Elector ran about twenty percent ahead of the least successful. Separate voting helped to produce the inexplicable straying of votes which lost one Elector for the dominant party in California and Ohio in 1892, California and Kentucky in 1896, and Maryland in 1904 and 1908. It was just another illustration of the way the party boss defeated the expectations of the reformers by making one concession and holding to the substance of power—in this case, the arrangement of the ballot paper.[23]

Although the palm must be awarded to the legislature of Kentucky for enacting the first Australian ballot law, generally the South was lagging. Ten states had not adopted the reform by 1892. Seven of the ten had belonged to the confederacy—Louisiana, Alabama, Georgia, South Carolina, North Carolina, Virginia and Florida—and Tennessee and Texas had passed laws only local in operation. By 1910, Georgia and South Carolina had still to adopt the reform and the laws of Tennessee and North Carolina were only local in operation. However some southern Mugwumps felt about electoral abuses in the big cities, many politicians were dragging their feet rather than face up to the problem of white illiteracy. As Professor William H. Glasson of Trinity College, North Carolina, editor of the *South*

[23] Allen, "Ballot Laws and their Working," 53–56.

97

Atlantic Quarterly, put it in 1909 before his own state had adopted the reform: "The Australian system did not lend itself to racial discrimination." He felt that as sophisticated "other methods" were now being used (presumably the new qualifications for the suffrage and the wide discretion of the registrars), the white voter should get the benefit of the reform, with an emblem and other concessions to illiterates.[24]

The quest for the Australian ballot had run its course by 1910. It was virtually complete. It had stimulated a number of other reforms, which led to the heart of the Progressive era. As John Wigmore had forecast in 1889, accurately it would seem: "The ballot-reform movement promises to have effects far wider than the mere achievement of a single reform. It is the opening of a road (perhaps the only road) to the whole field of political improvements."[25]

[24] Arthur C. Ludington, "Ballot Laws in the Southern States," *South Atlantic Quarterly,* IX (January, 1910), 21–34; William H. Glasson, "The Australian Ballot: why North Carolina should Adopt it," *ibid.,* VIII (April, 1909), 132–42; Ludington, *American Ballot Laws,* 84–88.

[25] Wigmore, *Australian Ballot System,* 56.

CHAPTER VI

This Spirit of Independency

Some day, not now, not in the heat of this campaign, but afterward, it may be not for years afterward, but some day, it will be seen that this spirit of independency is as much the need of the hour as the spirit which led men formerly into the Free Soil party. It is the growth of this spirit which shall make the issues change. . . . It is this spirit which at last shall lead parties, even if by unconscious steps, into the paths which shall divide the Union once more, not by sections but by ideas. . . . Happy, I know, are they who, with good conscience, can take part as partisans in the strifes of the hour. . . . But not less happy are they who at the call of conscience can leave all this and simply stand and wait.

(Seth Low, 1888)

Godkin, White and various others of the 'better element' have acted with unscrupulous meanness and a low, partisan dishonesty and untruthfulness which would disgrace the veriest machine heelers.

(Theodore Roosevelt, 1886)[1]

The Australian ballot in the United States was mainly due to the efforts of a distinct type of person commonly known as a Mugwump, and prominent from the liberal Republican bolt of 1872 until the Bull Moose called in 1912. A closer look at these earnest and dutiful people will make clearer what the reformer sought and why he sometimes failed.

The word Mugwump is derived from the Indian for a chief or great man, and according to the *Oxford English Dictionary* was already being used in 1832 as a jocular term for a great man or boss. It was widely used to describe those Republicans who bolted from their party after the nomination of James G. Blaine in 1884.

---

[1] *Address of the Hon. Seth Low before the Reform Club at Cooper Union, October 17, 1888* (Brooklyn, 1888), 35; Roosevelt to H. C. Lodge, November 1, 1886, in Morison ed., *Letters of Theodore Roosevelt*, I, 115.

The Australian Ballot:

The bolters of 1872 had been called independents and liberals, which were rather colorless terms for a people who have called political factions such names as Barnburners, Copperheads and Carpetbaggers. Mugwump seemed also to suggest a social type and an attitude to politics, as did "Goo-goo," an abbreviation of good government, in the 1900's. The word seemed to fit and was in time accepted by educated people of some means, people who particularly advocated civil service and ballot reform, and who scorned party regulars and precinct workers for their lowly and selfish aims.

The agitation in New York was led by the Commonwealth and City Reform Clubs and the Society for Political Education; by the *Nation* and *Evening Post* among the press; and by Richard R. Bowker, William M. Ivins and E. L. Godkin as individual members and publicists. The importance of the state in presidential politics and the dominance of her financial and publishing institutions in the late-nineteenth century ensured rapid and nation-wide attention.

The clubs were cause and effect. They catered to the needs of the growing number of well-educated, self-supporting professional and business men, especially in New York City. Bowker and Henry Holt were equally at home in the literary and business worlds. In the 1860's and 1870's, such men could establish their own publishing firms which became big incorporated "houses" in their own lifetimes. They had the means and inclination to lead an active social and public life, but without the means or pretension to nourish the conspicuous luxury of the contemporary "Four Hundred." By providing a meeting place and a program, the clubs thus encouraged more and more of the lawyers, publishers, journalists and others to reveal themselves and to use the clubs' backing for their own projects.

What were the main aims and characteristics of such men? They were essentially independent and pragmatic, pursuing specific reforms such as the Australian ballot, civil service and tariff revision. Like many Progressives, they were driven by a somewhat naive but determined belief that the common man was a fundamentally honest but thwarted elector, who could be stirred up and persuaded by speech and earnest tract to share their belief in the existence and evil of corruption and to demand honest and limited government. The cynical boss of the Progressive era called them Goo-goos because they could be passed off as respectable people who believed in good government and little else. Many Progressives, including Richard Welling, a club reformer and Godkinite who grew with the times, did urge wider social reforms to provide the basic and often boss-provided needs of the growing urban masses. But they still had much in common with more conservative reformers. Theodore Roosevelt has acquired a reputation as a realist and a leader who would enlarge the activities of government at home and abroad, yet he writes like a man who is fighting with the reader's conscience. As a speaker he throve on emotional language and forceful gestures. His realism consisted of a balance of ideals—to pursue efficiency with idealism; peace with righteousness; and collective action with individualism.[2]

The Mugwump as a social type figured prominently in the history of the Australian ballot. He was proud of his independence, seriousness and sense of duty. He could readily be derided as superior and genteel, even aristocratic. The type could flourish in Boston-Cambridge, where the old families comprised a tight social elite, and respected institutions such as Harvard University, the Massachusetts Historical Society and the Saturday Club perpetuated and gave it shape. A professional or amateur scholar was honored, doubly and trebly if he had family and means. Professor Andrews Norton married well and his son, Charles Eliot Norton, in turn held a Harvard chair. Henry Cabot Lodge's father had means, and the Cabots had arrived in 1630. Lodge first busied himself with scholarship, journalism and a possible academic career before seeking leadership of the state

[2] See Ch. V, fn. 7; Roosevelt, *Autobiography*, v-vi, 523–40, 575–81; George Haven Putnam, *Memories of a Publisher, 1865–1915* (New York, 1915), 171–72, 333–38. Putnam recalls pessimistically the popular response or lack of response to the educational activities of the reform clubs. The Foreword and discussion of Socialism and of peace illustrate from his *Autobiography* the above estimate of Roosevelt.

The Australian Ballot:

Republican party. In 1889, his sister-in-law married Brooks Adams, who in a few years would deliver his doom-laden thesis, *The Law of Civilisation and Decay*. The Adams brothers had means from their mother and the esteem due to two presidents of the United States through their father, who was himself prominent in politics and diplomacy. Richard Henry Dana, so prominent in the history of the Australian ballot, had a father and grandfather of some distinction and married Edith Longfellow, daughter of the noted poet and Harvard professor.

A Boston reformer like Norton grasped many filaments of the national life. Between 1864 and 1868, he edited the *North American Review* and gathered the means to set up Godkin as founder-editor of the *Nation*. He regularly corresponded with many public figures and wrote for the periodical press. He edited the works of two reformers from different generations, James Russell Lowell, who had been an ardent abolitionist, and George W. Curtis, who became first president of the National Civil Service Reform League in 1881 and a leading Mugwump bolter of 1884. In his academic life, he was professor of the history of art at Harvard from 1874 to 1898, a translator of Dante, and teacher of the great art critic, Bernard Berenson.

The Harvard roll also included the New York classmates, Richard Welling and Theodore Roosevelt, who had called the first meeting of the City Reform Club in his own home. In the sprawling metropolis, these clubs created the same ties as the Boston social system and enabled returning Harvard men to meet like-minded Columbia graduates such as William M. Ivins and Seth Low. Tulane University, the Cotton Exchange and the appropriate Krewes for the Mardi Gras festival performed the same function for the southern Mugwump in New Orleans. The reformers of Boston-Cambridge and New York also linked themselves with educated foreign liberals of fallen estate, such as the Anglo-Irishman, E. L. Godkin, and Carl Schurz and Henry Villard, two German victims of 1848. Villard married the daughter of the leading Boston abolitionist, William Lloyd Garrison, and in the 1870's, a fortuitous contact with German bondholders enabled him to join the ranks of the wealthy and oft-despised railroad promoters. He discreetly put up most of the money for purchase of the New York *Evening Post,* and Schurz, Godkin and Horace White were installed as editors. Godkin's weekly, the *Nation,* became a sister-journal, with Wendel Phillips Garrison as editor and little change in policy. In 1918, his nephew, Oswald Garrison Villard, sold his interest in the *Post* and assumed complete ownership and the editorial chair of the *Nation,* so linking the old with a new generation of reformers.

Many seemed to thrive on the strict and earnest regimen. Norton died in 1908 at the age of eighty-one, and had been a member of the Saturday Club for forty-eight years. His distant cousin and academic innovator, Charles W. Eliot, president of Harvard for forty years, died in 1926 at the age of ninety-two, and had been a member of the club for fifty-six years. Richard Henry Dana III died at the age of eighty, and Frederic Stimson at the age of eighty-nine. Of the New York liberals, Bowker died at eighty-five and Welling at eighty-eight. Mr. Richard S. Childs, at the age of eighty-five, is still an active chairman of the executive committee of the National Municipal League.

Harvard men, even Henry Adams, Stimson, Lodge and others who later acquired some reputation for scholarship, emphasized the importance of acquiring social poise and the manners and characteristics of a gentleman. It was no disgrace for a man to skimp the compulsory Latin recitations and finish down the list, if he followed his own bent and acquired a good name in the college. The mere grind, or "swot," to use the English vernacular, was an object of scorn despite his class mark. The fellow was doubtless a scholarship boy and a rebuke to president Eliot's *outré* ideas.[3]

The newcomers, rich or poor, native or immigrant, attracted by the growth and industry of Boston, were beginning to look for their own leaders and were less and less subject to the influence of the older families. A democracy tempered by respect was regarded by one Mugwump as the "perfect democracy" of

[3] Frederic J. Stimson, *My United States* (New York, 1931), 80, 191–92.

the early years of the republic. Along with his family capital and social standing, he inherited a strong obligation to take up reforms and public service. Although Dana could not hope to emulate his father who wrote a literary classic and stood against the redoubtable Ben Butler, he drafted laws and gave freely of his time. In 1864, a group of Cambridge teen-agers were planning a torchlight procession in support of Lincoln's candidacy. They adopted Dana's arrangement and elected the thirteen-year-old as captain, "which my family tradition," he explained in characteristic Mugwump fashion, "would not allow me to decline." The Massachusetts Reform Club, established in 1882, provided a gathering place for city and state politics. It included most of the Mugwumps and by 1890 was a powerful forum of independent opinion, with two hundred eighty-six members and a long waiting list.[4]

Independence was a main feature of the Mugwump outlook. A person who was public spirited and yet aloof was not likely to admire modern party organization and party loyalty. Richard Bowker took pride in the fact that he had been a "young scratcher" in 1879, a Republican bolter in 1884, and a Goldbug Democrat in 1896. In the interval, he had worked actively for Cleveland and tariff reform, and even described Protection as "the only serious menace to American liberty." Godkin and Schurz followed a similar course; and after a successful reunion with the Republican party, they fell out again by opposing Imperialism. Frederic Stimson attended Republican conventions until the bolt and then supported Cleveland; but he did not attend any more party conventions until 1900, when he supported the anti-Bryan Democrats. Dana wrote to Grover Cleveland shortly after his renomination in July, 1888, that he would support him for another term, just to push civil service reform. To another correspondent, he wrote that it was difficult to form their own party pledged to both civil service and tariff reform. The local civil

[4] *Ibid.*, 18–28; Perry, *Dana,* 31, 121–40; Blodgett, *Gentle Reformers,* 19–47; Geoffrey T. Blodgett, "The Mind of the Boston Mugwump," *Mississippi Valley Historical Review,* XLVIII (March, 1962), 620.

service reformers included protectionists, while some tariff reformers were prepared to combine with the spoilsmen to achieve
their aims. He added that the leaders of the Republican party had
long abandoned worthy causes and were a vested interest, opposed
to the civil service and the Australian ballot. Dana preferred to
support specific causes and pick candidates singly while holding
his traditional allegiance in reserve. This was also the attitude
of the meeting of independent Republicans who opposed the
Blaine nomination in 1884. Their resolutions declared that they
were divided over other questions and offices, but united in the
belief that the candidate was "unworthy of respect and confidence," and that his nomination superseded any other issue. They
added that Cleveland was no Copperhead but a supporter of civil
service reform, whose views on finance were acceptable to the
"best men" in both parties. This was only a recommendation,
as the conference laid on the table a motion to declare Cleveland
and Thomas Hendricks as their nominees for president and
vice-president. Carl Schurz opened their campaign in Brooklyn
on August 5, 1884, where Seth Low, one of the leading bolters,
was mayor. He addressed himself specifically to Republicans, and
asked them by their adverse votes to repair the dishonor done
to the party. As Cleveland became President by taking New
York state with a plurality of only 1,149, anyone who "scratched"
the national ticket could share the power of independence.[5]

Seth Low expressed the dilemma of many educated Mugwumps
over tariff revision in an informed and tightly argued address

[5] R. R. Bowker, *The Arts of Life* (New York, 1900), 16, 153–54, 189;
The Peoples Cause, June, 1889, 78; Stimson, *My United States,* 131–32;
Putnam, *Memories of a Publisher,* 180–91; Blodgett, "The Mind of the
Boston Mugwump," 633; Dana to Charles Eliot, October 20, 1887, Dana
Papers; Dana to Grover Cleveland, November 19, 1887, July 13, 1888,
Cleveland Papers; New York *Times,* July 23, August 6, 1884. The above
is Bowker's longest and most significant work, based on a systematic
theory of individualism. The "young scratchers" distributed Republican
tickets in 1879 with the name of Alonzo Cornell for governor blacked
through; they charged him with assessing customs house officers for the
party funds. Dr. Blodgett exaggerates the "moral grandeur" of the
Mugwump position; there were practical difficulties as Dana's letter to
Eliot indicated.

delivered in October, 1888. He believed in a limited Protection to assist new industries and would trust Republicans rather than their opponents to review the policy. Cleveland, whom he had supported in 1884, had shown exemplary courage in raising the issue squarely before his party and now before the people. The Republican platform and campaign, however, demanded a fight between the two opposed principles of Protection and Free Trade. As he believed that Protection had no permanent value but had to be steadily revised, he therefore reluctantly withdrew his support. Some day, he felt confident, the correct policy would emerge and "this spirit of independency" would be seen as the need of the hour, just as men had joined the Free Soil party when the cause looked hopeless. It was fine to join partisan battles, but "no less happy are they who at the call of conscience can leave all this and simply stand and wait."[6]

This is a characteristic Mugwump speech, balanced and pedagogic in tone, polished in style, characteristic of the speaker and the type. He consciously harks back to an earlier generation of idealists and to the origins of the Republican party. It reveals their lasting admiration for Cleveland. It urges the importance of ideas in the political process. His likely mentors are drawn from England, like the civil service reform itself. John Stuart Mill provided the argument in the United States and Australia that infant industries were an exception to the Free Trade rule. John Milton, a contemporary of the first Lows to settle in America, patiently submitting to his blindness, had said: "They also serve who only stand and waite."[7]

Their world of clubs and tracts was a different world from the saloon bar and door-knocker to which the ward boss was accustomed. The Society for Political Education in 1883 claimed one thousand four hundred members who received four tracts a year for the subscription of fifty cents. Tract twenty-seven, a

[6] See fn. 1.

[7] John Stuart Mill, *Principles of Political Economy: with Some of their Applications to Social Philosophy,* ed. W. J. Ashley (London, 1909), 916–26, 1002–03; John Milton, Sonnet XIX, Oxford Standard Authors ed., last line.

lengthy readers' guide to political, social and economic science, was published by Putnams for sale to the public at large. The City Reform Club was formed at an inaugural meeting at Theodore Roosevelt's residence in October, 1882. Soon afterwards, he had to attend the legislature in Albany. He resigned, and on his suggestion the club excluded any officeholders or political workers. Its main objects were to secure capable men and business methods in local governments, and to oppose partisanship. By March, 1883, it claimed three hundred fifty members who paid only an initiation fee of five dollars. The Commonwealth Club was founded in New York in December, 1886, and soon included among its members Bowker, Curtis, Godkin, Holt, Ivins, Schurz, Roosevelt, Villard, Welling, Worthington C. Ford, Elihu Root, Walter Hines Page, and president Andrew White of Cornell. Most members appeared to be journalists or lawyers. It was limited to two hundred fifty members, who paid an initiation fee of three dollars and an annual subscription of two dollars, plus the cost of the monthly dinner. The dinner meetings addressed by Ivins on money in elections were held at the Metropolitan Hotel on Broadway and cost one-and-a-half dollars without wine, which at the contemporary price level suggests solid comfort. Its object was simply "the discussion of political and economic questions," and members were committed only to civil service reform. There was no great financial barrier. What linked the club reformers were the Mugwump virtues of education, independence, and earnestness.[8]

Although he had the same social and intellectual pretensions, Theodore Roosevelt was developing his own political concept of "efficiency," and revealing a combative temperament. He could see little use for these independents. Men who remained in a permanent state of bolt were in effect partisans, and worse because hypocritical. In 1884, he had accepted the decision of the convention, but did not campaign. More and more he denounced

[8] Welling, *As the Twig is Bent*, 41–42, 53–54. This paragraph is also based on miscellaneous letters, lists and other material in the Bowker and Welling Papers, New York Public Library, Manuscript Division.

them with characteristic vigor, especially in his letters to Henry Cabot Lodge. Godkin was described as "a malignant and dishonest liar." When he stood unsuccessfully for mayor of New York in 1886 at the urgent pleading of the party leaders, he wrote that the New York *Evening Post* and the "better element" were backing Abram Hewitt, the Democratic candidate, "with unscrupulous meanness and a low, partisan dishonesty and untruthfulness which would disgrace the veriest machine heelers." As a Civil Service commissioner in 1889 and guest speaker to the National League, he frankly told them that he was aware of their criticism, but as a practical politician, he had a chance of making the victorious party keep its pledges.[9]

Although the Mugwumps despaired of such compromise, they felt that Roosevelt was sound at heart. In the last letter sent to his old friend E. L. Godkin, Charles Eliot Norton of Harvard described the recently assassinated President, William McKinley, as "that smug, canting, self-righteous servant of the Devil." Roosevelt, whatever his faults, had "a spirit of his own . . . at least the instincts and honesty of a gentleman."[10]

Roosevelt felt that the Mugwumps were not only hypocrites but also shrinking and snobbish creatures who scorned the lowly work of attending precinct meetings and cultivating the common voter. Such work would have shown them why the boss outlasted their scorn and tracts. He was *efficient,* one of Roosevelt's favor-

[9] Roosevelt to H. C. Lodge, August 12, 1884, November 1, 1886, December 27, 1888, October 11, 1892, October 3, 1895, in Morison ed., *Letters of Theodore Roosevelt,* I, 76–77, 115, 151, 292, 482; Hagedorn ed., *Works of Theodore Roosevelt,* XIV, 39–40, 88–92. Despite his statement, Roosevelt did make some speeches in the campaign of 1884. Presumably he did not criticize the benefits of independence; Massachusetts voted for him and a Democratic governor in 1904. In drawing a contrast between the Mugwumps and Roosevelt, it is relevant to note that Carter Harrison, five times mayor of Chicago between 1879 and 1893, and George McClellan, mayor of New York between 1903 and 1907 and later a Professor at Princeton, were also college men of good family, authors and avid readers, who relied on the much-criticized Democratic machines in their cities.

[10] Norton to Godkin, December 31, 1901, Godkin Papers, Houghton Library, Cambridge.

ite words. He understood and served the common man and gathered his vote which the intellectual club *flaneur* did not. Roosevelt perceived this fairly early in his career. In an article written in 1886 and previously quoted, he said, discussing the vexed question of patronage: "This fact does not of itself make the boss a bad man; there are several such I could point out who are ten times better fellows than are the mild-mannered scholars of timorous virtue who criticise them."[11]

The same point of view was put with a more finished turn of phrase by Curtis Guild in 1891, a prominent Boston journalist who was evidently a clubman himself:

> The struggles of conscience endured on caucus nights by a man who has settled down at the club to a long drink and the French illustrated papers are painful to witness. He is not quite sure that he is a Republican, and cannot therefore attend the Republican caucus. He has never attended and does not propose to attend the Democratic caucus. He is an independent who proposes to choose the better candidate. In other words, he will graciously condescend to assist in the chase after the party beaters have scared up the game. The possibility of his being forced to choose between a vulture and a turkey buzzard apparently does not occur to him.[12]

Richard Welling was a clubman who slowly perceived that a mere change in political machinery was inadequate. He felt that the club should serve the same functional purpose as the saloon and machine, and provide a meeting place, candidates, and an organization to back them. An active sportsman of six feet, three inches, determined and eagle-eyed, he plunged into a series of causes. By 1890, he was secretary-treasurer of the Commonwealth and treasurer of the City Reform Club. In 1894, he attended the initial meeting of the National Municipal League in Philadelphia and was helping to establish Good Government

[11] Hagedorn ed., *Works of Theodore Roosevelt,* XIII, 95. Compare with Schurz's more superficial description of a boss in an address to the National Municipal League in 1894, in Frederick Bancroft ed., *Speeches, Correspondence and Political Papers of Carl Schurz,* 6 vols. (New York, 1913), V, 214–26.

[12] Curtis Guild, "A Requisite of Reform," *North American Review,* CLII (April, 1891), 506.

Clubs around New York City. About the turn of the century, he decided that the boss was simply a go-between of the "needy rich" seeking franchises and favors, and the "grateful poor," who loyally offered their votes for his practical sympathy. The secret ballot did little to weaken his influence and ticket. Welling's most important activity in his own opinion was the movement to encourage the teaching of civics in schools. This began about 1904 with the support of John Dewey and other prominent people. As "the twig is bent," and as the teen-ager sees the effect of well-conducted elections and public meetings for himself, so Welling felt, he would become a good citizen. He was sufficiently stirred in 1932 to vote for Norman Thomas, the Socialist candidate, who resembled him physically and otherwise. Soon afterwards, the grim-faced old liberal hit the headlines to oppose some interference with his much-loved Central Park.[13]

Sometimes the Mugwumps joined with friendly radicals and partisans. The report of the first National Conference for Good City Government held at Philadelphia in January, 1894, which established the National Municipal League, included the names of many of the best-known reformers of the day. The president was James Carter, president of the City Club of New York; Welling represented one of the Good Government Clubs of the city, and Schurz the National Civil Service Reform Association. The list of sponsors included Charles F. Adams, Jr.; Norton and Dana from Boston; Godkin, White, Roosevelt and Abram Hewitt from New York; Henry C. Lea, the scholarly publisher from Philadelphia; and Richard T. Ely, the radical economist from the University of Wisconsin. The committee of the New York Ballot Reform League in 1896 included Bowker from the Reform Club; Schurz and Welling from the Commonwealth Club; and representatives from the West Side Republican Club; Republican

---

[13] Welling, *As the Twig is Bent, passim;* typescript in the Welling Papers, inscribed "about 1890" and entitled "The Need of Organisation in Municipal Reform." The City Reform Club was re-named and re-organized by Edmond Kelly in 1892 as the City Club. He tried but failed to attract Labor support. Forming Good Government Clubs was now one of their main activities.

Volunteer Association; City Reform Club; Manhattan Single
Tax Club; Lincoln Club; Excelsior Labor Club; and the Irish-
American Republican Club. The vice-presidents included
Chauncey Depew, Henry George, Carl Schurz, William M.
Ivins and Samuel Gompers.[14]

There is one man impossible to ignore in considering the
Mugwumps' outlook or their opinion of the Australian ballot
or anything else. He was Edwin Lawrence Godkin. He also
exercised an extraordinary influence over other editors and over
James Bryce, the English scholar, whose three-volume study of
The American Commonwealth has been an accepted authority on
American politics since it first appeared in 1888. Bryce wrote in
the course of their lengthy correspondence:

> I should have liked to say in the Preface how much more I
> am indebted to you than to any other source for the views
> I have formed, both to your letters and talk and to the *Nation*
> articles, but thought it would be more prudent not to do so
> because all the set of people whom you have been battling
> against all these years would at once lay hold of the state-
> ment and say (not without truth) that I was reproducing
> the *Evening Post* and Mugwumpism.

Now a wide new audience were shaking their heads at the
escapades of Boss Tweed and Dennis Kearney.[15]

[14] *Proceedings of the First National Conference for Good City Government* (Philadelphia, 1894); Welling, *As the Twig is Bent*, 49.

[15] Bryce to Godkin, October 22, 1888, Godkin Papers; Ogden, *Life and
Letters*, II, 230; Holt, *Garrulities of an Octagenarian Editor*, 287–88;
Villard, *Fighting Years*, 123; Stimson, *My United States*, 51. It is perhaps
characteristic of high-minded people that they are touchy about their
sincerity. Bryce had to write again in a soothing manner that he did
not mean to imply by the previous letter that Godkin was a political
encumbrance. Bryce to Godkin, January 24, 1889, Godkin Papers. I am
grateful for a note on the Godkin-Bryce letters from Mr. Edmund Ions of
York University, December 7, 1966. He says that Godkin's reply to
Bryce's letter of October 22, 1888 does not appear to be extant. I shall
not reproduce his comments further as the matter will be treated at length
in his forthcoming book on *Bryce and America*. Roosevelt told Lodge
that Godkin would not attend a dinner if he, Roosevelt, were present.
Roosevelt to Lodge, October 3, 1895, in Morison ed., *Letters of Theodore
Roosevelt*, I, 482.

The Australian Ballot:

Godkin's father was a Presbyterian clergyman of old Irish family who had been forced from his parish during the troubles of 1848. A Home Rule background and Queens College, Belfast drew him to the creed of Bentham and Mill. In 1853, when Godkin was only twenty-two, he wrote a history of Hungary which popularized the cause of Louis Kossuth and national revolt. Drifting between law and journalism in London, Godkin decided that the brash and malleable young republic across the Atlantic was a more favorable field for a gentleman of advanced opinions. He was admitted to the bar in New York in 1858 just before his marriage. The stirring issues of the Civil War and Reconstruction drew him back into journalism and the *Nation* was launched as a weekly in July, 1865. For the next thirty-five years he was a veritable institution, a stern Manchester radical who did not develop with his times.[16]

The *Nation* considered that the fight against the spoils system, protective tariffs and Imperialism concerned all classes of men. Although the arguments were sometimes specifically directed to Labor, the principles of classical political economy seemed more and more barren and useless for the laborer in an age of rapid industrialization and urban squalor. The classical theorists upheld free competition and the theory that there was only a limited fund available for wages. Trade Unions were acceptable because they enabled the workingman to bargain equally; but neither they nor their political supporters could upset the wages or hours determined in the marketplace. Following Mill, Godkin could only suggest that they set up cooperative workshops and add a profit factor to their wages. Like William Graham Sumner, the champion of the Spencerian doctrine of the survival of the fittest in social relations, Godkin was consistent. A protective tariff disrupted the market as much as a law for an eight-hour working day, and his disdain for the *nouveau riche* manufacturers who wanted it strengthened his opposition. In addition, he felt that Protection might encourage the masses to also use their votes to

[16] Ogden, *Life and Letters,* I, 11–12; Holt, *Garrulities of an Octagenarian Editor,* 282–95.

confiscate property, and so contained the germs of Socialism and the class struggle.[17]

Godkin's fears of Socialism were persistent. But such fears were often curbed by his analytical sense and zest for information, and he was never so emotional as to lose the grip of a pungent and readable style. For example, he gave a lengthy and objective summary of a French book on the Internationale, before concluding with a criticism of the Paris Commune. Another article showed keen interest in the piecemeal collectivism of the Australian colonies. Although he could ponder Socialism in the abstract, the nomination of William Jennings Bryan by the Democratic party in 1896 offered a serious challenge and roused him to anger. "Besides them the Populists are lamb-like and Socialists sucking doves," he wrote of the silverite majority. It was not just a matter of putting McKinley in, but of keeping Bryan, Ben Tillman, John Peter Altgeld and the "incendiary" hosts of "indescribables" and "repudiators" out.[18]

The voters ignored the windy rhetoric from the prairie by a large majority, even in traditionally Democratic New York City. But now came the lurid tales from Cuba, the war with Spain, and a rising tide of Imperialism which seemed the last straw. The letters that passed between Godkin and Norton from 1898 to 1901 are full of the despair of aging and tiring men, for whom the greed and clamor and slippery leadership of the day seemed the very antithesis of all they had fought for. Returning from a trip to England, Norton matched the mood of his old friend:

[17] Villard, *Fighting Years,* 119–22; Brooks, *New England: Indian Summer,* 117–18; *The Nation,* IV (April 25, 1867), 334–36, XII (May 25, 1871), 352–53, XIV (January 4, June 13, 1872), 12–13, 386–87. For a list of specimen articles, see Ogden, *Life and Letters,* II, 260–68.

[18] *The Nation,* XIV (January 4, 1872), 12–13, LXIII (July 16, 1896), 39, 42–43; "The Australian Democracy," *Atlantic Monthly,* LXXXI (March, 1898), 322–36. I feel insufficient attention has been paid to Godkin's style, which, at its satiric best, resembles that other genteel-born expatriate Irishman, George Bernard Shaw. It is common to regard Richard T. Ely and others as the wave of the future, and to imply that contemporaries were almost perversely ignoring them. When read side by side in a periodical with articles by Godkin, Sumner and David Wells, Ely appears flat, vague and deficient in argument.

"The same evil influences have been at work there as in America, and with the same ill result, the materialisation of the public temper, the vulgarisation of society, and the increase of jingo militarism."[19]

The comment of Van Wyck Brooks, who has written two brilliant and evocative studies of the New England mind, is equally applicable to the Mugwumps. "They could not understand," he states, "the vast, shambling new Republic, with its scandals, its corruption and its greed."[20]

Without spelling out details, a southern Mugwump, who was also responsible for the Australian ballot, has been mentioned. Is the label justified? John Parker, governor of Louisiana between 1920 and 1924, was the son of a planter and a president of the cotton exchange in New Orleans. In 1912, while vice-chairman of the Good Government League, he became a prominent figure in the national Progressive party and put that arch-Progressive, Hiram Johnson of California, into nomination as their candidate for vice-president. Walter Flower, who received the Citizens League nomination for mayor in 1896, was also the son of a planter and a president of the cotton exchange, and a graduate of Tulane law school.

Two of the most active leaders of the Citizens League, who were intimately connected with the adoption of the Australian ballot in Louisiana (the state being used for precise illustration), were Henry Dickson Bruns and Charles Janvier. Bruns was a leading ophthalmologist and president of the Louisiana Medical Society in 1895. He had been chairman of the Young Mens Democratic Association in 1888, when aged only twenty-nine, and led a large team of armed men watching the polls. Eight years later, he carried out similar work for the Citizens League. In future years, the National Municipal League, tariff revision and the Good Government League all claimed his attention. Charles Janvier, the president of an insurance company, had a busy year in 1896 when he was president of the League and King of Car-

[19] Norton to Godkin, July 21, 1900, Godkin Papers.
[20] Brooks, *New England: Indian Summer,* 141.

nival for the annual Mardi Gras festival. It is difficult to describe the active members of the League systematically. The press gave some details of twenty-one members of the League's legislative ticket. Of that group, fourteen were under forty years of age; six were graduates of Tulane law school; almost all belonged to a profession or an independent business; and few had any previous connection with politics except perhaps membership of the Young Mens Democratic Association. So the charge could be made in 1896 that the Citizens League were rich or "silk stocking" reformers. This they countered in the usual way by offering themselves as a mass movement to rescue the city. "Ten thousand men of mark and muscle march," thundered a front-page headline, along with stirring cartoons and references to the immortal spirit of September 14. The year was unnecessary for southerners, but for others this regular reference was to the race riots in New Orleans in 1874. The *Times-Democrat* heralded victory with the virtuous maid of Orleans holding aloft a sword and shield emblazoned with the potent magic monogram—"C. L."—while crushed underfoot was the serpent of "boodle" with severed head. The southern Mugwump was serious indeed. He shared the dedication of the eastern Mugwump to sound money, reform clubs and a righteous cause.[21]

In a suggestive chapter entitled "What Manner of Men," Professor George Mowry tried to draw a composite picture of the California Progressives, which might serve as a model by

[21] New Orleans *Daily Picayune,* April 12, 18, 1896; New Orleans *Times-Democrat,* April 22, 1896. After the party convention, the latter paper supported Bryan, the former continued to support sound money. On the youth of the southern Mugwump, Dr. Henry C. Dethloff says: "A comparison of available biographical sketches suggests that Populists averaged as much as fifteen to twenty years older than urban reformers." "Populism and Reform in Louisiana," 12. Much information in this chapter comes from many scattered sources including the standard bibliographical aids. The social *éclat* of Tulane University and certain carnival Krewes mentioned in describing the New Orleans Mugwump as a representative of the southern type is well known to locals, the dramatist, Tennessee Williams, and doubtless to sociologists who follow the methods of Dr. Lloyd Warner.

which to estimate Mugwumps and Progressives elsewhere. They tended to be young, eager, well-educated and of comfortable means. They were independent professional and business men, not dependent on politics or the large corporations for their livelihood. The local bosses and heelers called them "Goo-goos," or respectable people standing for good government and little else; and true or not, enough people believed it to make the jibe stick. The above details suggest that Mugwumps around the nation, in Boston, New York, New Orleans or San Francisco, were very much alike and had much in common with those reformers usually called Progressives.[22]

The more astute of the Mugwumps realized that they faced an unfortunate dilemma. If manhood suffrage and individual enterprise produced the boss and the trust, and if politicians believed in "waving the bloody shirt" and holding out the greasy palm, this was perhaps regrettable, but the necessary outcome of the nation's vital institutions. How and why should one combat it? The politicians reflected the people who sent them. An organized and competitive party of independents was self-contradictory. But surely, others felt, there were lessons to be found in history and America's own traditions which *compelled* one to combat it. Henry Adams, that constant intellectual seeker from an older Boston, more than once put his hand on the dilemma. It is caught most agreeably in the anonymous novel which he wrote in 1879 after his move to Washington. *Democracy: an American Novel* is written with his usual clarity and finesse, and with what can only be described as a cultivated sneer. Indeed, the satire is at times frankly humorous. Henry Holt immediately accepted his friend's manuscript and it found a large audience on both sides of the Atlantic.[23]

It is necessary to summarize the plot to explain a significant quotation. Bored alike by good works and easy living, Mrs. Light-

[22] Mowry, *California Progressives,* 86–104.

[23] (Henry Adams), *Democracy: an American Novel* (New York, 1880). Authorship was not fully confirmed until Henry Holt wrote his memoirs. *Garrulities of an Octagenarian Editor,* 136–39. For an Englishman's comment see Griffin, *The Great Republic,* 107.

foot Lee, a wealthy and still young New York widow, decides to
live in Washington and observe the very source and operation
of government. To her salon there come Senator Silas P. Ratcliffe of Illinois; Baron Jacobi, diplomat and *roué* from Bulgaria;
Schneiderkoupon of Pennsylvania, a subtle guardian of the tariff
and sound money; and the Washington lawyer Carrington, an
impoverished son of "ole Virginny." Though a bachelor and
from a different state, Ratcliffe instantly suggests the dominant
personality of the "Plumed Knight," James G. Blaine. He is
perturbed by the pending arrival of the President, a dull fellow
and his rival, who began life as a quarry laborer. By constantly
discussing his problems with Mrs. Lee, he flatters her desire for
influence. The President, variously known as "Old Granite"
and "The Stonecutter from the Wabash," hoped to check Ratcliffe, but is outsmarted and finds him indispensable in handling
patronage seekers and other chores uncongenial to his rustic soul.
Meanwhile, Carrington is pining for Mrs. Lee, and is loved in
turn by Sybil, her sister. To get rid of him and earn Madeleine
Lee's gratitude, Ratcliffe finds him an overseas post, and then
proposes marriage. The opportunity to make her own and her
sister's place secure is irresistible; but Carrington plays his trump
card and proves that Ratcliffe has received bribes. In a dramatic
scene, Ratcliffe urges for the last time the excuse of party success,
and shocked at his candid immorality, Mrs. Lee expels him from
the house. She muses bitterly that though fashionable society
might condemn, Ratcliffe's career is unaffected and nine-tenths
of the people will say she made a mistake to refuse him.

The dilemma is posed in an early conversation at her salon.

"I am asking Senator Ratcliffe," said she, "what is to become
of us if corruption is allowed to go unchecked." "And may
I venture to ask permission to hear Mr. Ratcliffe's reply?"
asked the Baron.
"My reply," said Ratcliffe, "is that no representative government can long be much better or much worse than the society
it represents. Purify society and you purify government. But
try to purify the government artificially and you only aggra-
vate failure."
"A very statesmanlike reply," said Baron Jacobi, with a formal

bow, but his tone had a shade of mockery. . . . "You Americans believe yourselves to be excepted from the operation of general laws. You care not for experience. I have lived for seventy-five years, and all that time in the midst of corruption. I am corrupt myself, only I do have the courage to proclaim it, and you others have it not . . . you gentlemen in the Senate very well declare that your great United States, which is the head of the civilized world, can never learn anything from the example of corrupt Europe. You are right . . . I do much regret that I have not yet one hundred years to live. If I could then come back to this city . . . the United States will then be more corrupt than Rome under Caligula; more corrupt than the Church under Leo X; more corrupt than France under the Regent."[24]

[24] (Adams), *Democracy*, 71–73.

CHAPTER VII

The Vote Market

New York has never had an approximately honest election.
(Paul Blanshard and Norman Thomas, 1932)

This political Boss touched a sense of gratitude so deep
that he could count on the votes of the grateful poor even
though the ballot was secret, and so our problem was:
the "needy rich" and the "grateful poor," almost like a
machine gifted with perpetual motion.
(Richard Welling, 1942)

Which leads up to our definition of a politician—a citizen
who knows what he is doing on election day!
(Richard S. Childs, 1952)[1]

It was a great achievement in both the United States and Great
Britain to have swept away the encrusted habits and vested
interests which had sustained the old electoral system. The
conduct of elections now attracts little attention from political
scientists. It is assumed that they are fair and orderly, and an
accurate expression of the popular will. It is otherwise with
psephology, the study of the electors' behavior. At this very
moment, scores of questionnaires are being drawn up or conveyed
from door to door, and tabulations will then be made of how
a sample of voters reacts to certain issues and how such factors
as their age, sex, income and education affect their choice of
party.

Several political bosses in the major cities would have laughed
at such an assumption in the 1920's and 1930's. The election of
William Scott Vare, the Republican boss of Philadelphia, to the
United States Senate in 1926 earned him the distinction of a

[1] Paul Blanshard and Norman Thomas, *What's the Matter with New
York: a National Problem* (New York, 1932), 79, 83–87; Welling, *As the
Twig is Bent*, viii–ix; Childs, *Civic Victories*, 37.

119

special investigation by that body. In three hundred ninety-five divisions in Philadelphia, the number of ballots exceeded the registered voters. While a political scientist, J. T. Salter, watched, 166 of 177 voters at a polling place asked a full-time party worker to "assist" them. Eventually, Vare was unseated for excessive expenditures.[2]

A canvas of twenty-three Chicago precincts immediately after the elections of April, 1926, revealed that forty-four percent of the votes cast were fraudulent—that is, forty-four percent of the voters listed in the poll books were dead, had shifted residence, or had not in fact voted. The elections of 1928 were marred by roving bands of thugs who intimidated voters, kidnapped workers for the opposition, and shot one candidate dead. If the conduct of the local police only slightly justified the strictures of the grand jury, they could be easily fobbed off. The mayor, William H. Thompson, preferred to drive "the treason-tainted textbooks" out of the schools. In 1930, a reporter described conditions in the still notorious first ward:

Hinky Dink's Province Holds an Election

Democracy and prosperity were triumphant in the South State Street district of the First Ward yesterday. The instructed ballot took care of democracy and 50 cents a vote, with no arbitrary limit on repeaters, provided the prosperity. Everybody had a good time and the general comment was "a quiet, orderly election."

Last August Michael (Hinky Dink) Kenna, for forty years boss of the First Ward, appeared before County Judge Jarecki to proclaim his "the cleanest ward in the city." A reporter, therefore, spent yesterday in the State Street lodging house district, where as many as 130 free men are registered from the same address, to observe a clean ward at the polls.

The first citizen who took any notice of the reporter was Mr. Patrick Sheehan—born in Boston but raised in the old country—who wore a long black overcoat, a cap with a broken bill, a white Lewis for Senator badge, and a tomato nose. . . .

"Have you voted son?" inquired Mr. Sheehan, extending a long quivering hand.

[2] Harris, *Election Administration,* 322–40; Salter, *Boss Rule,* 30, 149; Overacker and West, *Money in Elections,* 33–34.

"Do you want to make 50 cents?" He was told that a vote had been cast in another precinct.

"Well, I voted once in the 27th ward and then voted here," he replied. "But that was all right, I voted in the 27th ward for my son. He's in Minnesota. . . ." For three hours Mr. Sheehan was observed sauntering from one citizen to another, always with the same query, "Want to make 50 cents?" And most of them did. The four polling places in the two blocks between 8th and 10th streets were constantly attended by from twenty-five to one hundred of the 25 cents a day lodgers throughout the day, and it was a simple matter to single out one of them, and watch him vote two or three times, often in the same polling place.

The old abuses of bribery and repeating were still prevalent here. It is also significant to note the four polling places in two blocks, providing a well-paid chore for the heelers.[3]

Ballot reformers still found it easier to gather evidence of fraud than to prosecute successfully or to win elections. In July, 1936, the St. Louis *Post-Dispatch* exposed heavy padding of the rolls in Kansas City, Missouri, by the Democratic machine led by "Tom" Prendergast. Yet Kansas City was among those which had adopted the council-manager system, the goal of municipal reformers. The paper used its own staff and resources, and began legal proceedings in that city and throughout the state. However, the machine's ticket was still returned at the election two years later. A reform ticket was eventually successful, so cleansing the black sheep of the council-manager list.[4]

[3] Harris, *Election Administration,* 340–60; Chicago *Daily Tribune,* November 1, 5, 1930. The newspaper on another page reported that on the same day four had been killed and two wounded during the elections in Kentucky. Bearing in mind conditions in contemporary Chicago, it seems laughable and a patent red-herring that Thompson should begin an article written in 1928 as follows: "Treason-tainted text-books were a big issue in the Chicago mayoral campaign last Spring." He was referring to anglicized textbooks which were following reputable scholars and making points now regarded as commonplace. William Hale Thompson, "Shall we Shatter the Nation's Idols in School Histories?" *Current History,* XXVII (February, 1928), 619–25.

[4] Richard S. Childs to the author, March 2, 1966; Silas Bent, *Newspaper Crusaders: a Neglected Story* (New York, 1939), 32–39. Joseph Pulitzer, an active Liberal who bought the paper in 1878, did much to shape its traditions.

The Australian Ballot:

What of the present? Jack Harrison Pollack's description of ballot-stuffing and the registration of lodging-house "ghosts" might have been written in 1856, instead of 1956. In 1960, there was criticism of "The Vote Market" which secured the return of mayor Richard Daley in Chicago and which may have been the crucial factor in the state of Illinois and in the close presidential contest of that year. It was alleged that scores of fraudulent absentee ballots were cast in Arkansas in November, 1964, and many were peddled in the state hospitals. But coercive methods were not needed in Boston to secure the election of James Curley while still under indictment for mail fraud. Past experience indicates the limited results of tinkering with the machinery of elections. While precinct captains can still get jobs on the public payroll and spend their copious free time in winning friends, and while the ballot is still so large and complicated, abuses and poor candidates will persist. Perhaps further changes in the system of elections are desirable and possible, if the reformers do not resurrect the fetish of independency and do not expect too much of the average voter. There is clear need to introduce a short ballot and the civil service organization of the election officials. These changes would make the adoption of the Australian ballot complete. By the same token, the Australian system has shortcomings, and a party designation on the ballot and other changes could be copied with profit from the United States.[5]

[5] Jack Harrison Pollack, "They'll Steal your Vote," *National Municipal Review*, XLV (July, 1956), 322–27; Harold Baron, "The Vote Market," *The Nation*, CXCI (September 3, 1960), 109–12; Richard S. Childs to author, March 2, 1966 enclosing extract from *National Municipal Review*, November, 1965; Jerome Bruner and Sheldon Korchin, "The Boss and the Vote: Case Study in City Politics," *Public Opinion Quarterly*, X (no. 1, 1946), 1–23. For irregularities and intimidation in several southern states as part of a system of a dominant faction in a one-party section in the 1940's, see V. O. Key Jr., *Southern Politics in State and Nation* (New York, 1949), 443–62. Advocates of civil service conduct of elections include Peel, *Political Clubs*, 155–59; Salter, *Boss Rule*, 262–70; Blanshard and Thomas, *What's the Matter with New York*, 91; and of the short ballot, Childs, *Civic Victories*, 3–91, 283–90. Joseph Harris, a leading authority, drew up a list of fifty specific reforms in *A Model Election*

The comparison of political systems may be fruitful, but never exact. Only a simpleton would expect to find or demand the Australian or British type of party discipline in the United States. Sectional and ethnic loyalties often transcend those of class; and local radicals may dislike the same program when administered from Washington. To indicate how loose are party ties, Dwight Eisenhower and Barry Goldwater carried Louisiana in 1956 and 1964 respectively, although the proportion of registered Democrats was ninety-nine percent, and no Republican sat in the state legislature between 1898 and 1964. Nor does the presence of two Representatives in a house of one hundred five indicate a revival. At the elections held in November, 1962, there were twenty-six states balloting for both a United States Senator and a governor. In no less than twelve, the party of the two winners did not coincide, and in three others, one victor heavily outran the other.[6]

It has been shown how independency was carried to an extreme by the cross-filing law of California, and how the voters' behavior was influenced by the arrangement and form of the ballot devised by the party leaders. Similarly, in many states, the large and cumbersome blanket ballot is deliberately designed to encourage heedless party conformity. Most states follow the Indiana or party column arrangement. Some have additional features. The sample ballot furnished by Louisiana for the presidential election of November, 1960, is a facsimile of the face of the voting machine as the voter confronts it in the booth. It is arranged in party columns, each headed by a distinguishing emblem, and the voter can vote a

---

Administration System (National Municipal League, 1961), which emphasize civil service, the short ballot and permanent registration. One other possible reform should be noted. There is no official tally of the votes cast for the presidential Electors by any federal agency. The national Network Election Service, set up for the election of 1964, can provide not only a speedy and near-unanimous return, but its staff can provide a further, independent check on the count. This desirable result is due not to reformers and legislators, but to the commercial spirit allied with commonsense.

[6] *Report of the Secretary of State* (Baton Rouge, 1964); further information from contemporary periodicals. The standard of "heavily" is eight percent.

straight ticket with one pull of the large lever adjacent to the emblem. There were three columns—the Democrat, under a rooster; the Republican, under an elephant; and the States' Rights under the emblem of the Statue of Liberty. The offices to be elected were the ten presidential electors; a United States senator; a United States representative; members of two state boards; five judicial offices; four local offices; and a school board of five. In addition, the electors had to vote separately on fifty-five proposed constitutional amendments, for Louisiana has the dubious distinction of having the lengthiest constitution of any state. In fact, the edition with amendments up to November, 1954, and an index contains six hundred ninety-one pages. Most of the amendment proposals referred to zoning, taxation, and the powers of agencies in single parishes. All this paraphernalia required a large blanket ballot measuring twenty-seven by forty-three inches, and the word "blanket" can now mean both "inclusive" and "blanket-sized." Such a large ballot is likely to produce what some political scientists call electoral fatigue. The first-named presidential electors gathered a combined total of 807,891 votes, whereas only 334,455 voted on the fifty-fifth amendment.[7]

It is possible to give many other examples. The voters in Chicago in November, 1930, were handed a big ballot, a smaller ballot and two special ballots for the bond issues. The sample printed in the press listed a United States senator and a state ticket of nine; thirty-two Cook County offices; fifteen local judicial offices; and three legislative offices by district, or fifty-nine in all. The voters also had to decide on fourteen bond issues, three amendments to the state constitution, and three separate and cleverly worded proposals dealing with the Eighteenth Amendment. The Democrats and "wets" swept the state in a landslide, so it is not certain how many dogcatchers and sewer commissioners relied on Senator James H. Lewis' coattails. A generation later, in November, 1948, a voter in Cuyahoga County, Ohio, which includes Cleveland, had to decide on seventy-five offices and propositions, and in Wayne County,

[7] Sample ballots and recent *Reports* were furnished by the office of Mr. Wade O. Martin Jr., Secretary of State for Louisiana.

Michigan, which includes Detroit, on fifty-five offices and propositions in five separate ballots. The main ballot in Wayne County
measured eighteen by twenty-four inches, and included twenty-one
state representatives chosen at large and eighteen other offices on
seven separate tickets. Not surprisingly, nine-tenths of the voters
put an "X" mark in the circle under the party emblem at the head
of a ticket. Running for re-election was the state treasurer. In a
sample of voters interviewed just before the elections of 1950,
ninety-six percent could not give his name, although he had been
elected four times.[8]

According to recent textbooks, thirty states have a party column
and eighteen an office block arrangement of their ballot papers.
The two recently admitted states of Hawaii and Alaska have com-
mendable short ballots with an office block arrangement.

Some political scientists however claim that this sort of argument
is misguided. Two of the leading behaviorists, Dr. Angus Campbell and Dr. Warner Miller of the University of Michigan Survey
Research Center, found that the ballot arrangement encouraged
a straight ticket vote, but the strongly identified partisan was much
less affected by a different arrangement than the independent or
weak partisan. Their conclusion, which has been widely repeated,
is that the latter were following the line of least effort by choosing
a party ticket or choosing at random according to the arrangement.
They were therefore not the model citizens of folklore, that is of
the Mugwump tradition. In his last book, the late V. O. Key
criticized several such propositions of the behaviorists. He found
that switching voters, or weak partisans, and new voters could be
anything up to two-fifths of the electorate. He also found that in
their education standards, votes and answers to questions they revealed compared with strong partisans not ignorance and indifference but a consistent and valuable judgment of the issues. Whatever
the research may reveal, it is undeniable that many party leaders
in the past have used the arrangement of the ballot to fight a
rearguard action against the implications of ballot reform. The

[8] Chicago *Daily Tribune,* November 2, 3, 1930; Childs, *Civic Victories,*
27–28, 291–95.

raison d'être of a political party is to wield power. They are concerned with election results, not strong or weak motivation or the other categories of the academic political scientist. The Mugwumps were in error to suggest that an intelligent and informed citizen might not persistently vote a straight party ticket. The modern pundit is in error to suggest that the most worthy citizen should not try to obviate electoral fatigue and simplify the operation in the party column states when confronted with a blanket ballot filled with strange names, trivial offices and self-perpetuating constitutional amendments.[9]

When Arthur Ludington compiled his digest of *American Ballot Laws* in 1911, twenty-one states had passed laws permitting the use of voting machines. In 1934, only nine states and certain localities in six other states were actually using them. But by the presidential elections of 1952, it was estimated that forty percent of all votes were cast by machine. On the face of it, a machine is fast and accurate in counting and proof against abuse. A lever closes a curtain and conceals the voter. He then depresses other levers corresponding to each candidate or proposition, or a large lever set for a party column vote. But the whole record of ballot reform indicates that the form can be preserved while the substance is lost; and that elaborate laws for the registration of voters, the conduct of elections and the use of ballot boxes may count for little. The machine has to be read, and so can be mis-read or mis-set before the votes have been cast. California, with her tradition of independency and bipartisan reform, still clings to a paper ballot, rubber stamp and numbered stub. Whatever method is used, the four principles of the Australian ballot are retained. It is provided by the state; a facsimile ballot containing the names of all nominated candidates is set into the machine which excludes other ballots; and the structure serves as an enclosed booth.[10]

[9] Angus Campbell and Warner Miller, "The Motivational Basis of Straight and Split-ticket Voting," *American Political Science Review*, LI (June, 1957), 299–300; V. O. Key Jr., *The Responsible Electorate: Rationality in Presidential Voting, 1936–60* (Cambridge, 1966).

[10] Ludington, *American Ballot Laws*, 202–07; V. O. Key Jr., *Politics, Parties and Pressure Groups*, 4th. ed. (New York, 1958), 696–98;

If some people allege that the machines can be rigged, why have not the election officials discovered it? The strict and lengthy laws dealing with the selection of officials and their pay indicate that an election is usually regarded as a well-paid chore for a large number of party workers. In Louisiana, for example, there is a Board of Supervisors of Election in each parish, consisting of the registrar and two persons appointed by the governor. In Orleans parish, the governor appoints one supervisor and also appoints the registrar. Members receive twenty-five dollars for the election and for each day they hear registration appeals. The Boards appoint three commissioners and one clerk for each polling place, as far as practicable choosing equally from the parties authorized to make nominations. They are paid, as are the deputy-sheriffs, between twelve-and-a-half dollars and twenty dollars a day, depending on the number of voters. The commissioners thus have an inducement to increase the vote, and the law also provides a loose "assistance" clause which can be abused in the interests of partisanship, for partisans they are. The law also creates a framework for a chain of command leading down from the governor to two loyal Democrats of his faction at each polling place.[11]

In 1929, Joseph Harris, author of two thorough surveys of electoral practice, said categorically that nine-tenths of the frauds were perpetrated by the officials themselves or with their knowledge and consent. Officials who display their allegiance and wear their badges in the polling place are provided with a dangerous temptation. It is still possible to stuff ballots and falsify returns. Furthermore, their great numbers help to swell the costs of reg-

---

Blanshard and Thomas, *What's the Matter with New York*, 81–82.

"The count of votes is a physical check of each ballot-paper. Machines have been considered from time to time, but due mainly to the fact that we have some 10,000 polling places in the Commonwealth and a preferential system of voting, machines have not been adopted." Mr. F. L. Ley, Chief Electoral Officer of the Commonwealth of Australia, to the author, October 18, 1962.

[11] Louisiana, *Revised Statutes*, 7 vols. and supplement (Baton Rouge, 1950), II, Title 18, "Elections," Sections 554–55, 732. The pay has been checked against the amended versions issued in 1960.

istration and elections. The number of voters using each precinct polling place about 1930 varied from one thousand four hundred six in New Haven down to one hundred thirty-seven in San Francisco. In New York City, the average cost of registration was seventy-one and eight-tenths cents a voter, and gathered only forty-three percent of those eligible; in Milwaukee, it was eight and one-tenth cents and gathered seventy percent. The average cost of elections in New York was one dollar thirty-six cents a vote cast, and in Milwaukee was fifty-six cents, or less than half as much. The obvious cause of the discrepancy was that Milwaukee had a system of permanent registration and an electoral-office staff belonging to the civil service, whereas New York did not.[12]

The practice in Milwaukee has been steadily increasing. The loss of the old, face-to-face contact which exists in a small community led to personation and other abuses, and some of the growing cities in the mid-nineteenth century began to introduce a system of advance registration of qualified voters. It was assumed that a fresh list gathered periodically would be the least fraudulent; but the contrary has been shown time and time again, apart from the additional costs of paying party workers and printers to man the offices on registration day and produce the rolls. The system of permanent registration was first used in Boston in 1896. The principle is that a voter, having personally applied and been enrolled, stays on the list until he dies, moves, or persistently fails to vote. The Louisiana law of 1952 is a recent example, although it is confined to the city of New Orleans and to the general elections. The existing register was made permanent, subject to stringent checking. Court, health and other officials and even lodging-house keepers must file regular returns so that deceased persons and other ineligibles might be erased from the list. The registrar and police must make a periodic canvas of houses and act upon complaints.

---

[12] Harris, *Registration of Voters,* 255–84, 361; Harris, *Election Administration,* 429–30. His figures are not gathered for uniform years, hence the phrase, "about 1930." The author's personal observation is limited to a primary election in New Orleans. The officials were wearing the badges of the various candidates including those handing out the ballot papers, and a table inside the room displayed the candidates' publicity material.

The registrar must keep proper office hours, a card index of voters and applications, and up-to-date equipment. The records are open to the public. Above all, the registrar in New Orleans has a permanent staff under the state civil service and is less dependent on temporary partisans.[13]

Many areas not only persist with periodic registration laws, but also have stringent residence qualifications. It is common to require the voter to have one year's residence in the state, six months in the county, and thirty days in the precinct where he votes. In Louisiana until 1960, the terms were two years, one year, and three months respectively. These requirements are a relic of the old days when it was necessary to establish local contact and rely on challenges at the polling places to detect fraud. The result is that thousands are disfranchised in a nation whose very traditions encourage mobility. In some states, due to the strict residence and other qualifications, only about two-thirds of the adult population are enrolled, and it is considered a very good poll if three-quarters of those enrolled actually vote.[14]

Thus the Australian ballot has not fulfilled some of the expectations of the pioneers, and its working is still obstructed by the party machines. It has ended direct bribery and intimidation; but some indirect bribery through fees and electoral service remains. It has not opened doors for poor, independent and third party candidates, which were among the objectives of George and Ivins. Rather, it has led to a cumbersome, blanket ballot handed out by "politically designated" officials. It sustains a host of professional

[13] Harris, *Registration of Voters*, 274-84; Louisiana, "Elections," Ch. I, Sections 224-54. Personal application in the South also serves other purposes, as the registrar interprets "good character" and other items in the extensive list of qualifications for the franchise in the above law. Sections 31-42. This is now subject to federal intervention under the Voting Rights Act of 1965.

[14] Constitution of Louisiana, Article VIII, Section 1. The proportion of registered voters to the population of voting age of Louisiana in 1960 was just under two-thirds. California presumably does not practice systematic disfranchisement in the southern manner, but has a heavy immigration. Her proportion of voters to available population in 1960 was just over two-thirds, or about three million people available and unregistered.

politicians to furnish the candidates and conduct the registration and elections. There are still frequent allegations of miscounting, repeating and other abuses. Two feasible reforms suggest themselves—the short ballot, and an electoral office under the civil service, which means a few, important offices on the ballot, and an impartial control of the elections.[15]

Further improvements in machinery and appeals to virtue will not by themselves remove corruption. Some of the Progressives concluded that the nineteenth-century reformers had made this mistake, and they decided that there would be less incentive to abuse the electoral system in order to secure franchises and favors if the public utilities were owned by the city governments. In more recent years, the boss's influence over the voters has been weakened by laws restricting immigration and by the superior benefits of impersonal, regular, government-administered social services over his spasmodic, "charitable" activities.[16]

Congressional ethics and campaign costs became a live issue in the press and periodicals early in 1967 when attempts were made to unseat or de-rank Representative Adam Clayton Powell. It was widely suggested that other politicians had hazy standards about gifts and conflicts of interest. Above all, the huge costs and hidden financing of campaigns might introduce substantial conflicts of interest and obligations to be repaid, and so weaken representative democracy. There are legal limits on the expenditures of candidates and interstate political committees, but private committees who pick up the bills without the candidate's "knowledge" and most primary elections, which may be the decisive elections, are unaffected. Alexander Heard, the leading authority on *The Costs of Democracy,* estimated that the total cash outlay for all campaigning at all levels in 1952 was one hundred forty million dollars. The figures must be much higher now as television time is used more extensively. To say that the figure is only one-tenth of one percent of the national income or is less than this outlay on gambling or

[15] The phrase is used by Peel, *Political Clubs,* 155–59.
[16] Lincoln Steffens, *The Autobiography of Lincoln Steffens* (New York, 1931), 492–93.

that outlay on advertising provides some perspective, but little justification. Costly elections give an unfair advantage to the very rich or to corporate wealth, as in the days before the Australian ballot, when the candidates were assessed by the parties for the costs of the election. The Australian ballot provides a precedent for the suggestion made by Theodore Roosevelt and by others in more recent years that the campaigns should be subsidized by public money. However, Congress has persistently refused to adopt such reforms or even to draw attention to the matter of corruption and ethics except to find some scapegoat from time to time such as Oakes Ames in 1872, William Scott Vare in 1929 and Powell in 1967.[17]

In the course of examining the faults of reformers, some of them put forward a theory of corruption. The search occupies many pages of the *Autobiography* of the "muckraking" journalist, Lincoln Steffens, published in 1931. Richard Welling discerned a perpetual movement between the "needy rich" and the "grateful poor." Perhaps this is a statement of general application or perhaps something more elaborate is required.[18]

Corruption in politics is the misuse of public office or function for private profit. The British Corrupt Practices Act of 1883 and similar American legislation stigmatized bribery of voters and other electoral abuses as corrupt practices, for they are commonly a one-sided and fraudulent means of gaining office and part of a system of corruption. It is impossible to stop isolated individuals from offering money to a humble policeman if he will tear up a parking ticket; but if corruption is widespread and requires important public decisions, if it becomes a system, a boss or intermediary may well appear to deal with the requests and ensure the results. In a representative democracy he will try to manipulate the elections, but if checked by reforms such as the direct primary and the Australian ballot, the conditions may still permit him to secure the return of his candidates in a relatively fair election.

[17] Alexander Heard, *The Costs of Democracy* (Chapel Hill, 1960).
[18] Steffens, *Autobiography*, 357–627; Welling, *As the Twig is Bent*, viii–ix.

The Australian Ballot:

The following is put forward as a tentative, general statement. Where certain conditions exist such as a large number of poor and ignorant voters, the ability of a government to provide a variety of individual favors, and lax standards among officials, there is a tendency to corruption. These conditions existed in the United States in the late-nineteenth century, and in diminishing force in the twentieth century. These conditions are brought forward to explain why corruption is widespread in newly independent countries today.[19]

On the other hand, there are certain features unique to the United States. To gather and reward his party workers, the boss could utilize a vast amount of patronage and at bottom the resources of a wealthy, industrialized country. The long, blanket-sized ballot encouraged ignorant voting and organized activity to provide the candidates. The Jacksonian tradition was averse to expertise in government. Some analysts claim that the American people have a distinctively acquisitive outlook, but ostentatious display and the purchase of a seat in the legislature as badges of success is hardly confined to the United States.[20]

There are also distinctive features in the modern, newly independent or "developing" countries. The degree of illiteracy, poverty and temporary housing is much more apparent than it ever was in the United States, which poses practical difficulties in devising an accurate register of voters and a usable form of ballot paper. Many countries were former colonies. They lack trained native officials, and their leaders in the course of the struggle for independence were often accustomed to treat the law with disrespect. The disposal of vast amounts of international aid provides a temptation unknown in the nineteenth century.[21]

Having given the warning that changes should do more than

[19] T. E. Smith, *Elections in Developing Countries* (London and New York, 1960), 227; Sir Ivor Jennings, *The Approach to Self-government* (Cambridge, 1956), 59–84.

[20] Peter Odegard claims that corruption in the United States is due at bottom to her distinctive pecuniary values. Seligman and Johnson eds., *Encyclopaedia of the Social Sciences*, IV, 454.

[21] Jennings, *Self-government*, 59–84.

improve the mere machinery of voting, it is still submitted that
the Australian ballot as an American reform is not yet complete.
The system could also be improved in the land of its origin. That
the Commonwealth Electoral Act should still ignore the presence
of political parties and not require party designation on the ballot
papers seems completely unrealistic. A distinctive feature of
Australian elections is party workers standing the distance required
under the law from the polling place with their colored "How to
Vote" cards. As voting is compulsory and the ballot paper contains names only, they are kept busy. It might be more beneficial
if the money and effort expended were instead spent on providing
information during the campaign itself. Party pre-selection ballots
in Australia are quite unofficial and in practice confined to a few
party stalwarts as in the palmy, pre-primary days of the American
boss. The Victorian branch of the Australian Labor Party has
recently abolished them, and the state executive of the party now
selects the candidates. It is possible that other branches and the
other parties might gradually follow suit. About half the American
states now register the voter with a party affiliation, and use this
roll to conduct a closed, direct and official primary election. The
turnout may be larger than the general election. Some use a consolidated primary, and the voters select their allegiance in the
booth. Australians might not welcome party registration, optional
voting and such loose tests of membership or affiliation. Others
may suggest that the party chieftains in Australia have become so
complacent and unwilling to educate the electorate that some drastic
changes are long overdue. Perhaps an official and well-publicized
primary might encourage more people to join a party. It could be
held in a set month of the second year of the life of the parliament
with some alternative provision when the Prime Minister or
Premier asks successfully for a dissolution. The voter's name could
be checked off against lists furnished by the parties and this might
avoid the more public commitment of registration by party.

To criticize the reform is not to decry the notable achievement
of Chapman, Dutton and Nicholson in Australia, and Dana,
George, Ivins, Cleveland and all the other people who actively

promoted it in the United States. That there are always people ready to brush aside the formalities of fair and secret voting is shown by the following extract. The occasion was a loyalty investigation launched by a committee of the state senate at the University of Oklahoma in February, 1941.

> Senator Joe Thompson: "Whom did you vote for in the last election?" Professor Mueller replied, "I thought the secret ballot in this country made it unnecessary to tell whom you vote for." To this evasion Thompson retorted, "Don't you think as a matter of good conscience and since you are a teacher in a state institution you should not hide behind the Australian Ballot." Mueller obediently replied, "I voted for Roosevelt."[22]

The implications are highly dangerous—that a state employee including school and university teachers has no privacy in voting, or anything else. The nineteenth-century Liberal is often criticized for his snobbish and self-righteous attitude, but in opposing the Thompsons of his age, he showed a genuine and eternal passion.

This anecdote perhaps demonstrates also that the laws and practices governing the conduct of elections are not a dry and isolated subject, but are vital for the whole democratic process everywhere. In the words of the Universal Declaration of Human Rights, 1948, Article 21, 3:

> The will of the people shall be the basis of the authority of the government, this will shall be expressed in periodic and genuine elections which shall be by universal and equal suffrage and shall be held by secret vote or by the equivalent free voting procedures.

[22] Cited in James A. Robinson, *Anti-sedition Legislation and Loyalty Investigations in Oklahoma* (Norman, 1956), 27.

BIBLIOGRAPHY

A. *Manuscripts:*

Bidwell, John, Dictation, 1891. Given to Hubert Howe Bancroft and a clerk. Extract provided by the Bancroft Library, Berkeley.

Bowker, Richard Rogers, Papers, 1880–1900. Unclassified letters and publications and trivia. Manuscript Division, New York Public Library.

Cleveland, Grover, Papers, 1887–92. Selected letters. Manuscript Division, Library of Congress.

Dana Family Papers, 1887–89. Selected letters and folder on Australian ballot of Richard Henry Dana III. Massachusetts Historical Society, Boston.

Donnelly, Ignatius, Papers, 1890–92. Microfilm reels provided by Minnesota Historical Society, St. Paul.

George, Henry, Papers, 1880–92. Newspaper files, publications, unclassified letters and notes. Manuscript and Economic Divisions, New York Public Library.

Godkin, E. L., Papers, 1865–1900. Classified letters. Houghton Library, Cambridge.

Welling, Richard W. G., Papers, 1882–92. Unclassified letters, minute books and notes. Manuscript Division, New York Public Library.

Williams, Timothy Shaler, Papers, 1889–1890. Selected letters. Manuscript Division, New York Public Library.

B. *Official Documents:*

Commonwealth of Australia, *Commonwealth Electoral Act,* 1918–61.

Great Britain, "Report of the Select Committee on Parliamentary and Municipal Elections," *Sessional Papers, House of Commons,* 1868–69, VIII.

Great Britain, "Papers Relative to the Operation of the System of the Ballot in the Colonies," *Sessional Papers, House of Commons,* 1871, XLVII, 317.

Hansard's *Parliamentary Debates,* Third Series, volumes CLVI, CCI–CCX, 1860, 1870–72.

135

Bibliography

Louisiana, *Acts Passed by the General Assembly*. Baton Rouge, 1896.

Louisiana, *Report of the Secretary of State*. Baton Rouge, 1892 *et seq*.

Louisiana, *Revised Statutes*, 7 vols. and supplement. Baton Rouge, 1950.

Massachusetts, *Journal of the House of Representatives* and *Journal of the Senate*. Boston, 1888.

New York, *Public Papers of David B. Hill, Governor*. 7 vols. Albany: The Argus Company, 1885–92.

United States, Bureau of the Census, *Thirteenth Census of the United States: 1910. Abstract with Supplement for Louisiana*. Washington: Government Printing Office, 1913.

Victoria, *Government Gazette*, March 26, 1856. Act 19, Vic. No. XII. Melbourne: Government Printer, 1856.

C. *Newspapers and Periodicals:*

Boston *Daily Advertiser*, 1888–89.

Chicago *Daily Tribune*, 1891, 1894, 1930.

Detroit *Free Press*, 1885, 1887, 1889.

Harper's Weekly, New York, 1871, 1887–92.

London *Times*, 1872.

Melbourne *Argus*, 1851, 1855–56, 1881.

The Nation, I–LXII. New York, 1865–96.

New Orleans *Daily Picayune*, 1896–98, 1912.

New Orleans *Times-Democrat*, 1896–98, 1912.

New York *Times*, 1884–96.

Public Opinion, II–XIV. New York, 1887–92.

Review of Reviews, III–IV. New York, 1891.

St. Louis *Post-Dispatch*, 1889.

San Francisco *Alta California*, 1854–56, 1889–91.

San Francisco *Daily Evening Bulletin*, 1891.

Sydney *Daily Telegraph*, 1890.

Washington *National Economist*, 1889–93.

D. *Pamphlets:*

Address of the Hon. Seth Low before the Reform Club, Cooper Union, October 17, 1888. Brooklyn: Publisher unknown, 1888.

Bibliography

(Bowker, Richard Rogers), *Electoral Reform*. Economic Tracts, No. 24. New York: Society for Political Education, 1889.

Denison, S. C., *Is the Ballot a Mistake?* London: J. Ridgway and Sons, 1838.

Ivins, William Mills, *Electoral Reform: the History of the Yates-Saxton Bill—the Question Stated*. New York: Publisher unknown, 1888.

———, *On the Electoral System of the State of New York*. Reproduced from the 29th Annual Report of the Proceedings of the New York State Bar Association. Albany: Publisher unknown, 1906.

(Johns, Fred?), *Australian Ballot: Pioneered by South Australia*. Place and Publisher unknown, 1910?

Universal Suffrage and Vote by Ballot in Australia . . . by an Old Colonist. London: P. S. King, 1867.

Vote by Ballot Society, *Tracts on the Ballot: Number Five*. London: Publisher unknown, 1855.

E. *Memoirs, Diaries, and Correspondence:*

Childs, Richard S., *Civic Victories: the Story of an Unfinished Revolution*. New York: Harper and Brothers, 1952.

Cleveland, Grover, *Writings, and Speeches of Grover Cleveland*. Edited by George F. Parker. New York: Cassell Publishing Company, 1892.

Dana, Richard Henry, "Sir William Vernon Harcourt and the Australian Ballot Law," *Proceedings of the Massachusetts Historical Society*, LVIII (June, 1925), 401–18.

Grote, George, *Minor Works of George Grote, with Critical Remarks on his Intellectual Character, Writings, and Speeches*. Edited by Alexander Bain. London: J. Murray, 1873.

Holt, Henry, *Garrulities of an Octagenarian Editor: with Other Essays Somewhat Biographical and Autobiographical*. Boston: Houghton Mifflin and Company, 1923.

Howe, Frederic C., *Confessions of a Reformer*. New York: Charles Scribner's Sons, 1925.

Kipling, Rudyard, *Letters of Travel, 1892–1913, and Other Sketches. Works,* 31 vols. Bombay ed. London: Macmillan and Company, 1913–38. XXVII.

137

Bibliography

Powderly, Terence V., *The Path I Trod*. Edited by Harry Carman *et al*. New York: Columbia University Press, 1940.

Putnam, George Haven, *Memories of a Publisher, 1865–1915*. New York: G. P. Putnam's Sons, 1915.

Roosevelt, Theodore, *An Autobiography*. New York: The Macmillan Company, 1913.

Roosevelt, Theodore, *Letters of Theodore Roosevelt*, 8 vols. Edited by Elting E. Morison *et al*. Cambridge: Harvard University Press, 1951–54.

Schurz, Carl, *Speeches, Correspondence and Political Papers of Carl Schurz*, 6 vols. Edited by Frederick Bancroft. New York: G. P. Putnam's Sons, 1913.

Steffens, Lincoln, *The Autobiography of Lincoln Steffens*. New York: Grosset and Dunlap, 1931.

Stimson, Frederick J., *My United States*. New York: Charles Scribner's Sons, 1931.

Villard, Oswald Garrison, *Fighting Years: Memoirs of a Liberal Editor*. New York: Harcourt, Brace and Company, 1939.

Welling, Richard W. G., *As the Twig is Bent*. New York: G. P. Putnam's Sons, 1942.

F. *Books:*

Aaron, Daniel, *Men of Good Hope: the Story of American Progressives*. New York: Oxford University Press, 1951.

(Adams, Henry), *Democracy: an American Novel*. New York: Henry Holt and Company, 1880.

Albright, Spencer D., *American Ballot*. Washington: American Council for Public Affairs, 1942.

Bass, Herbert J., *I am a Democrat: the Political Career of David Bennett Hill*. New York: Syracuse University Press, 1961.

Beard, Charles A., and Shultz, Birl E., eds., *Documents on the State-wide Initiative, Referendum and Recall*. New York: The Macmillan Company, 1912.

Bent, Silas, *Newspaper Crusaders: a Neglected Story*. New York: McGraw-Hill Book Company, 1939.

Blanshard, Paul, and Thomas, Norman, *What's the Matter with*

Bibliography

New York: a National Problem. New York: The Macmillan Company, 1932.

Blodgett, Geoffrey T., *The Gentle Reformers: Massachusetts Democrats in the Cleveland Era.* Cambridge: Harvard University Press, 1966.

Bowker, Richard Rogers, *The Arts of Life.* Boston: Houghton Mifflin and Company, 1900.

Brooks, Robert C., *Corruption in American Politics and Life.* New York: Dodd, Mead and Company, 1910.

Brooks, Van Wyck, *New England: Indian Summer, 1865–1915.* New York: E. P. Dutton and Company, 1940.

Bryce, James, *American Commonwealth,* 2 vols. 2nd ed. New York: Macmillan and Company, 1911.

Bullock, Edna D., ed., *Short Ballot.* White Plains, New York: The H. W. Wilson Company, 1915.

Dickens, Charles, *Posthumous Papers of the Pickwick Club.* London: Chapman and Hall, 1837.

Donnelly, Ignatius, *Caesar's Column: a Story of the Twentieth Century.* Edited by Walter B. Rideout. Cambridge: Belknap Press and Harvard University Press, 1960.

Eaton, Allen H., *Oregon System: the Story of Direct Legislation in Oregon.* Chicago: A. C. McClurg and Company, 1912.

Evans, Eldon Cobb, *A History of the Australian Ballot System in the United States.* Chicago: The University of Chicago Press, 1917.

Fleming, Edward McClung, *R. R. Bowker: Militant Liberal.* Norman: University of Oklahoma Press, 1952.

Frary, Donald Page, and Seymour, Charles, *How the World Votes: Democratic Development in Elections,* 2 vols. Springfield, Massachusetts: C. A. Nichols Company, 1918.

Gibson, Florence, *Attitudes of the New York Irish towards State and National Affairs, 1848–92.* New York: Columbia University Press, 1951.

Goldman, Eric, *Rendezvous with Destiny: a History of Modern American Reform.* New York: Vintage Books, 1956.

Griffin, Sir Lepel Henry, *The Great Republic.* New York: Scribner and Welford, 1884.

Hanham, H. J., *Elections and Party Management: Politics in the Time of Gladstone and Disraeli.* London: Longmans, 1959.

Bibliography

Harris, Joseph P., *Election Administration in the United States.*
Washington: The Brookings Institution, 1934.
——, *A Modern Election Administration System.* 4th ed. New
York: National Municipal League, 1961.
——, *Registration of Voters in the United States.* Washington:
The Brookings Institution, 1929.
Hays, Samuel P., *The Response to Industrialism, 1885–1914.* Chi-
cago: Chicago University Press, 1957.
Hazen, Evelyn, *Cross Filing in Primary Elections,* mimeographed.
Berkeley: Bureau of Public Administration, 1951.
Heard, Alexander, *The Costs of Democracy.* Chapel Hill: Uni-
versity of North Carolina Press, 1960.
Hicks, John D., *The Populist Revolt: a History of the Farmers'
Alliance and the People's Party.* Minneapolis: The University
of Minnesota Press, 1931.
Hofstadter, Richard, *Age of Reform: from Bryan to F. D. R.*
New York: Alfred Knopf, 1955.
Holmes, Frank R., *Minnesota as a State, 1870–1908.* New York:
The Publishing Society of Minnesota, 1908.
Howard, Perry, *Political Tendencies in Louisiana, 1812–1952.*
Baton Rouge: Louisiana State University Press, 1957.
Ivins, William Mills, *Machine Politics and Money in Elections in
New York City.* New York: Harper and Brothers, 1887.
Jennings, Sir W. Ivor, *Appeal to the People.* Cambridge: Cam-
bridge University Press, 1960.
——, *Approach to Self-government.* Cambridge: Cambridge
University Press, 1956.
Kales, Albert M., *Unpopular Government in the United States.*
Chicago: University of Chicago Press, 1914.
Key, V. O., Jr., *Politics, Parties and Pressure Groups.* 4th ed.
New York: Crowell, 1958.
——, *The Responsible Electorate: Rationality in Presidential
Voting, 1936–60.* Cambridge: Harvard University Press,
1966.
——, *Southern Politics in State and Nation.* New York: Alfred
Knopf, 1949.
Ludington, Arthur C., *American Ballot Laws, 1888–1910.* Educa-
tion Department Bulletin No. 488. Albany: University of the
State of New York, 1911.

Bibliography

Mann, Arthur, *Yankee Reformers in the Urban Age.* Cambridge: Belknap Press and Harvard University Press, 1954.

Marquand, John P., *The Late George Apley: a Novel in the Form of a Memoir.* Boston: Little, Brown and Company, 1937.

McCombie, Thomas, *History of the Colony of Victoria, from its Settlement to the Death of Sir C. Hotham.* Melbourne: Publisher unknown, 1858.

Morley, John, *Life of William Ewart Gladstone,* 3 vols. New York: The Macmillan Company, 1903.

Mott, Frank Luther, *A History of American Magazines,* 4 vols. Cambridge: Harvard University Press, 1938–57.

Mowry, George, *California Progressives.* Berkeley: University of California Press, 1951.

O'Brien, Conor Cruise, *Parnell and his Party.* Oxford: The Clarendon Press, 1957.

Ogden, Rollo, *Life and Letters of Edwin Lawrence Godkin,* 2 vols. New York: The Macmillan Company, 1907.

O'Leary, Cornelius, *Elimination of Corrupt Practices in British Elections, 1868–1911.* Oxford: The Clarendon Press, 1962.

Ostrogorski, M., *Democracy and the Organisation of Political Parties,* 2 vols. Frederick Clarke tr. New York: The Macmillan Company, 1902.

Overacker, Louise, and West, Victor, *Money in Elections.* New York: The Macmillan Company, 1932.

Parker, George F., *Recollections of Grover Cleveland.* New York: The Century Company, 1909.

Peel, Roy V., *Political Clubs of New York City.* New York: G. P. Putnam's Sons, 1935.

Perry, Bliss, *Richard Henry Dana, 1851–1931.* Boston: Houghton Mifflin Company, 1933.

Reid, T. Wemyss, *Life of the Right Honourable William Edward Forster,* 2 vols. London: Chapman and Hall Limited, 1888.

Robinson, James A., *Anti-sedition Legislation and Loyalty Investigations in Oklahoma.* Norman: University of Oklahoma Bureau of Government Research, 1956.

Salter, John Thomas, *Boss Rule: Portraits in City Politics.* New York: McGraw-Hill Book Company, 1935.

Bibliography

Serle, Geoffrey, *Golden Age: a History of the Colony of Victoria, 1851–61.* Melbourne: Melbourne University Press, 1963.

Seymour, Charles, *Electoral Reform in England and Wales: the Development and Operation of the Parliamentary Franchise, 1832–85.* New Haven: Yale University Press, 1915.

Smith, T. E., *Elections in Developing Countries.* London: Macmillan Company, 1960.

Stead, W. T., *Satan's Invisible World Displayed: or Despairing Democracy.* New York: R. R. Fenno and Company, 1897.

Sutherland, Alexander, contrib. ed., *Victoria and its Metropolis,* 2 vols. Melbourne: McCarron, Bird and Company, 1888.

Watson, Thomas E., *People's Party Campaign Book, 1892. Not a Revolt: it is a Revolution.* Washington: National Watchman Publishing Company, 1892.

Westgarth, William, *The Colony of Victoria.* London: Sampson, Low, Son and Marston, 1864.

Wigmore, John Henry, *Australian Ballot System as Embodied in the Legislation of Various Countries.* 2nd ed. Boston: Boston Book Company, 1889.

Wilcox, Delos F., *Government by all the People: or the Initiative, the Referendum, and the Recall as Instruments of Democracy.* New York: The Macmillan Company, 1912.

Williamson, Chilton, *American Suffrage: from Property to Democracy, 1760–1860.* Princeton: Princeton University Press, 1960.

Woodward, C. Vann, *Origins of the New South, 1877–1913.* Baton Rouge: Louisiana State University Press, 1951.

Woodward, James A., *American Politics: Political Parties and Party Problems in the United States.* Rev. ed. New York: G. P. Putnam's Sons, 1924.

Zornow, William F., *Kansas: a History of the Jayhawk State.* Norman: University of Oklahoma Press, 1957.

G. *Articles:*

Allen, Philip Loring, "Ballot Laws and their Working," *Political Science Quarterly,* XXI (March, 1906), 38–58.

———, "Multifarious Australian Ballot," *North American Review,* CXCI (May, 1910), 602–11.

Bibliography

Baldwin, Simeon E., "Early History of the Ballot in Connecticut," *Papers of the American Historical Association,* IV (October, 1890), 407–22.

"Ballot Reform Practically Accomplished," *Century Illustrated Monthly Magazine,* XXXIX (January, 1890), 472–73.

Baron, Harold, "Vote Market," *The Nation,* CXCI (September 3, 1960), 109–12.

Bernheim, A. C., "Ballot in New York," *Political Science Quarterly,* IV (March, 1889), 130–53.

Binney, Charles Chauncey, "Australian Ballot System," *Lippincott's Monthly Magazine,* XLIV (September, 1889), 381–88.

———, "Merits and Defects of the Pennsylvania Ballot Law of 1891," *Annals of the American Academy of Political and Social Science,* II (May, 1892), 751–71.

Bishop, Joseph B., "Genuine and Bogus Ballot Reform," *The Nation,* LII (June 18, 1891), 491–93.

———, "Secret Ballot in Thirty-three States," *Forum,* XII (January, 1892), 589–98.

———, "Successful Ballot Laws," *The Nation,* XLIX (October 17, 1889), 304.

Blodgett, Geoffrey T., "Mind of the Boston Mugwump," *Mississippi Valley Historical Review,* XLVIII (March, 1962), 614–34.

Bruner, Jerome, and Korchin, Sheldon, "Boss and the Vote: Case Study in City Politics," *Public Opinion Quarterly,* X (No. 1, 1946), 1–23.

Campbell, Angus, and Miller, Warner E., "Motivational Basis of Straight and Split-ticket Voting," *American Political Science Review,* LI (June, 1957), 293–312.

Clinton, Harris J., "Compulsory Voting Demanded," *North American Review,* CXLV (December, 1887), 685–86.

Dana, Richard Henry, "Australian Ballot System of Massachusetts," in *Proceedings of the Atlantic City Conference for Good City Government* (New York: National Municipal League, 1906), 349–62.

———, "Practical Working of the Australian System of Voting in Massachusetts," *Annals of the American Academy of Political and Social Science,* II (May, 1892), 733–50.

Daniel, Lucia Elizabeth, "The Louisiana People's Party," *Lou-*

Bibliography

isiana Historical Quarterly, XXVI (October, 1943), 1055–1149.

Destler, Chester McA., "Western Radicalism, 1865–1901: Concepts and Origins," *Mississippi Valley Historical Review,* XXXI (December, 1944), 133–68.

Finch, Edward R., "Fight for a Clean Ballot," *Independent,* LXVIII (May 12, 1910), 1021–26.

"Further Electoral Reform," *Century Illustrated Monthly Magazine,* XXXIX (February, 1890), 633–34.

George, Henry, "Bribery in Elections," *Overland Monthly,* VII (December, 1871), 497–504.

———, "Money in Elections," *North American Review,* CXXXVI (March, 1883), 201–11.

Glasson, William H., "Australian Ballot: Why North Carolina Should Adopt it," *South Atlantic Quarterly,* VIII (April, 1909), 132–42.

Godkin, E. L., "Australian Democracy," *Atlantic Monthly,* LXXXI (March, 1898), 322–26.

———, "Republican Party and the Negro," *Forum,* VII (May, 1889), 246–57.

Gross, Charles, "Early History of the Ballot in England," *American Historical Review,* III (April, 1898), 456–63.

Grubb, Edward B., "A Campaign for Ballot Reform," *North American Review,* CLV (December, 1892), 684–93.

Guild, Curtis, "A Requisite of Reform," *North American Review,* CLII (April, 1891), 506–08.

Holls, Frederick W., "Compulsory Voting," *Annals of the American Academy of Political and Social Science,* I (April, 1891), 586–614.

Ingalls, John J., "A Fair Vote and an Honest Count," in *The Republican Party: its History, Principles and Policies.* Edited by John D. Long (New York: The M. W. Hazen Co., 1888), 323–38.

Jenks, Jeremiah W., "Money in Practical Politics," *Century Illustrated Monthly Magazine,* XLIV (October, 1892), 940–52.

Julian, George W., "Abuse of the Ballot and its Remedy," *International Review,* VIII (May, 1880), 534–45.

Bibliography

Kennan, George, "Holding up a State," *Outlook*, LXXIII (February 7, 14, 21, 1903), 277–83, 386–92, 429–36.

LaFollette, Robert, Jr., "Adoption of the Australian Ballot in Indiana," *Indiana Magazine of History*, XXIV (June, 1928), 105–20.

Ludington, Arthur C., "Ballot Laws in the Southern States," *South Atlantic Quarterly*, IX (January, 1910), 21–34.

———, "Present State of the Ballot Laws in the United States," *American Political Science Review*, III (May, 1909), 252–61.

Mason, Alfred Bishop, "How to Bring Public Sentiment to Bear upon the Choice of Good Public Officials: through the Primaries," *Proceedings of the First National Conference for Good City Government* (Philadelphia: National Municipal League, 1894), 186–90.

McCook, J. J., "Alarming Proportion of Venal Voters," *Forum*, XIV (September, 1892), 1–13.

McWhinney, Grady, "Louisiana Socialists in the Early Twentieth Century: a Study in Rustic Radicalism," *Journal of Southern History*, XX (August, 1954), 315–36.

Moore, George Henry, "Notes on Tything-men and the Ballot in Massachusetts," *Proceedings of the American Antiquarian Society*, new series, III (April, 1884), 81–91.

Neale, R. S., "H. S. Chapman and the 'Victorian' Ballot," *Historical Studies*, XII (April, 1967), 506–21.

Pitchell, Robert J., "Electoral System and Voting Behaviour: the Case of California's Cross-filing," *Western Political Science Quarterly*, XII (June, 1959), 459–84.

Pollack, Jack Harrison, "They'll Steal your Vote," *National Municipal Review*, XLV (July, 1956), 322–27.

Redpath, James, "Electoral Reform," *North American Review*, CXLV (October, 1887), 451–54.

Remsen, Daniel S., "Fusion of Political Parties," *Annals of the American Academy of Political and Social Science*, VIII (July, 1896), 32–49.

Rice, Allen Thorndike, "Next National Reform," *North American Review*, CXLIII (December, 1886), 628–42.

Rightmire, W. F., "Alliance Movement in Kansas: Origins of the

People's Party," *Kansas State Historical Society Collections,* IX (1906), 1–8.

Roalfe, William R., "John Henry Wigmore: Scholar and Reformer," *Journal of Criminal Law, Criminology and Police Science,* LII (September, 1962), 277–300.

Romero, Sydney James, "The Political Career of Murphy James Foster, Governor of Louisiana, 1892–1900," *Louisiana Historical Quarterly,* XXVIII (October, 1945), 1129–1243.

Saxton, Charles, "Changes in the Ballot Law," *North American Review,* CLII (June, 1891), 753–56.

Saxton, Charles, *et al.,* "New Method of Voting," *North American Review,* CXLIX (December, 1889), 750–56.

Scott, Ernest, "History of the Victorian Ballot," *Victorian Historical Magazine,* VIII (November, 1920, May, 1921), 1–14, 49–62.

"Secret Voting and Parliamentary Reform," *Edinburgh Review,* CXII (July, 1860), 93–266.

Thompson, J. M., "Farmers Alliance in Nebraska: Something of its Origins, Growth and Influence," *Proceedings and Collections of the Nebraska State Historical Society,* X (1902), 199–206.

Wakefield, Edward, "Australasian Ballot System," *Forum,* VIII (October, 1889), 148–58.

Wigmore, John H., "Ballot Reform: its Constitutionality," *American Law Review,* XXIII (September–October, 1889), 719–32.

———, "A Summary of Ballot Reform," *The Nation,* XLIX (August 29, 1889), 165–66.

"Voting Power of Ignorance," *Century Illustrated Monthly Magazine,* XXXIII (March, 1887), 806–07.

H. *Miscellaneous:*

Appleton's Annual Encyclopaedia and Register of Important Events. New York: D. Appleton and Company, 1889–92.

Gosnell, Harold F., "Ballot," and Odegard, Peter, *et al.,* "Corruption," in *Encyclopaedia of the Social Sciences,* 15 vols. Edited by E. R. A. Seligman and Alvin Johnson (New York:

The Macmillan Company, 1930–35), II, 410–12, IV, 447–54.

Roosevelt, Theodore, *Works,* 20 vols. Edited by Herman Hagedorn. New York: Charles Scribner's Sons, 1926.

Serle, Percival, "Henry Samuel Chapman," *Dictionary of Australian Biography,* 2 vols. (Sydney: Angus and Robertson, 1949), I, 158–60.

Spofford, A. R., "Ballot," in *Cyclopaedia of Political Science, Political Economy and of the Political History of the United States,* 3 vols. Edited by J. J. Lalor (New York: C. E. Merrill and Company, 1888–90), I, 197–99.

I. *Unpublished Studies:*

Dethloff, Henry C., "Populism and Reform in Louisiana." Unpublished Paper furnished by the author, 1967.

Ferkiss, Victor S., "Political and Economic Philosophy of American Fascism." Unpublished doctoral dissertation, University of Chicago, 1954.

Fredman, L. E., "The Bigler Regime." Unpublished master's thesis, Stanford University, 1959.

Small, Milton M., "Biography of Robert Schilling." Unpublished master's thesis, University of Wisconsin, 1953.

INDEX

Index